Here There Be Monsters:
The Legendary Kraken and
the Giant Squid

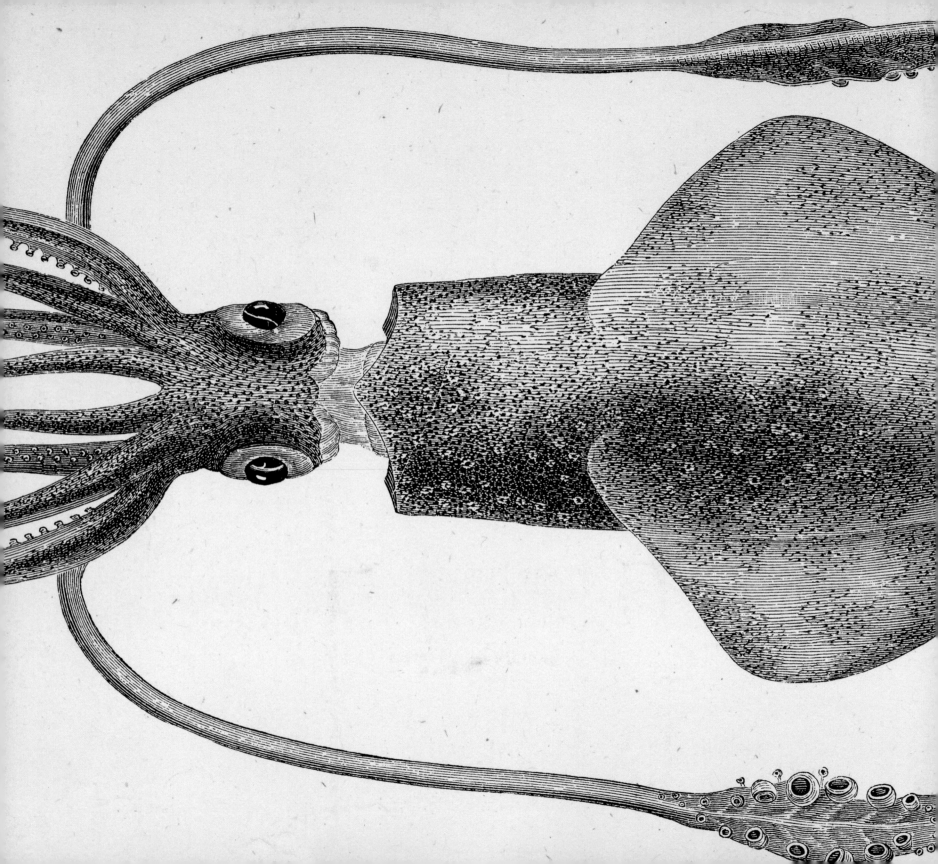

HERE THERE BE MONSTERS

*The Legendary Kraken
and the Giant Squid*

HP Newquist

Houghton Mifflin

Houghton Mifflin Harcourt

Boston   New York   2010

Houghton Mifflin is an imprint of Houghton Mifflin Harcourt Publishing Company.
www.hmhbooks.com
The text of this book is set in Minion.
Photo credits appear on page 71.

Library of Congress Cataloging-in-Publication Data
Newquist, H. P. (Harvey P.)
Here there be monsters : the legendary kraken and the giant squid / HP Newquist.
p. cm.
ISBN 978-0-547-07678-2
1. Kraken—Juvenile literature. 2. Giant squids—Juvenile literature. I. Title.
QL89.2.K73N49 2010
594'.58—dc22
2009045246

Manufactured in China
LEO 10 9 8 7 6 5 4 3 2 1
4500218381

To my parents, who let me watch
"Creature Feature"—no matter
what time it was on.

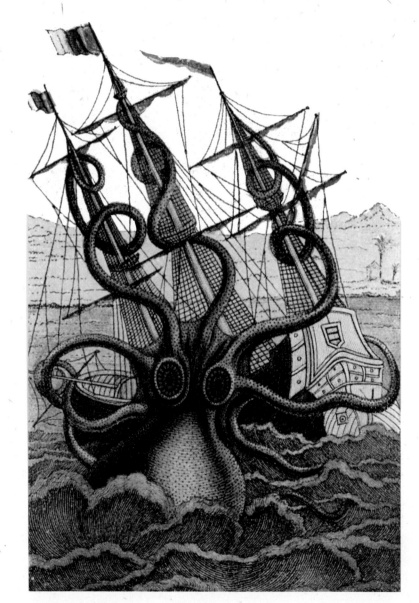

Prologue

The legends of a nightmarish creature living deep in the ocean were created hundreds of years ago, during a time when ships sailed in search of new lands, not always knowing what they would find or where they would end up. There were mysterious things, unseen things, that lurked under the surface of the water. And monsters were rumored to wait for the passing of a solitary ship to feed their hunger . . .

Imagine that you are on one of those ships, thousands of miles from the nearest land, and surrounded by nothing but water.

It is late at night and the world around you is utterly dark. There are fifty other people on the ship, but they are all asleep, most of them below deck. Tonight it is your turn to sit on the deck and watch the water and the sky. It is your duty to stay awake and look for anything that might affect your voyage: a sudden storm, a pod of whales, or a pirate ship creeping up in the distance.

Even though you should be in school back home, your parents have sent you off to sea because the owner of the shipping company needs crew men—even kids—to help on the ship. He will pay the money directly to your mother and father when and if the ship returns safely to your town.

Thankfully, all is quiet. The full moon reflects brilliantly off the ocean, although everything turns black whenever a cloud passes overhead. Then you cannot even see your hand when you hold it in front of your face.

The only sounds you hear are the slapping of the water against the sides of the boat and the creaking of the masts as they tilt side to side in the night. Everything is so still, and the boat is moving so slowly, that you feel like you're being rocked to sleep. It's so hard to stay awake. Your eyelids begin to droop and your head begins to nod. If you could only sleep for a moment . . .

Suddenly, something slams violently against the side of the boat. You jump to your feet, your heart racing. It sounded as if the ship hit a huge rock, but there is no land for thousands of miles in any direction.

There is silence for a moment. Then it happens again. The boat shudders. But this time, the deck under your feet tips downward. It feels like something is grabbing the ship and trying to pull it into the water. You run to the side and look over the railing, but you can't see anything. There is nothing to light the waves; the moon has slipped behind a cloud.

Then, through the inky blackness, you see something rise up from the rippling sea. It is ghostly and round, and it gets brighter as it nears the water's surface.

It is an eye.

The eye seems to be glowing, and it looks right up at you. It is bigger than any eye you've ever imagined—so big that it can't be real. It is almost as big as the captain's wheel, two feet across. It does not blink.

As you stare at the impossible eye, you hear a slithering, dripping sound—something heavy and wet slides by you. You look down and see a long dark tentacle reach out of the water and feel its way across the deck. Its suckers are white and moist, and they seem to squish as they attach themselves to the wood of the boat.

The tentacle looks like a giant python, curling and twisting, black and glistening. It snakes across the deck, making a clicking sound as it gropes about in the darkness. You wonder how a smooth, slithery arm can make hard grating sounds, like metal nails scratching at a door.

Then the moon shines through the clouds and you see that each of the hundreds of suckers on the slimy tentacles has a sharp rotating claw inside it. The claws stick out like rows of hooks—and each one is looking for something to grab, something to pull into the cold water. Something to eat.

More slithering snakes—arms and another tentacle—reach out from the ocean and wrap around the ship's railing, like gigantic fingers clutching a tiny toy. The boat lurches, and you suddenly know, deep down in your brain, that this monster is going to pull you and everyone else on board down into the ocean.

The giant eye comes closer and part of a head rises out of the water. There is a mouth, a dark hole slurping in the water, and it makes a chewing sound, like teeth chattering against one another.

One of the sucker-filled arms grabs your foot. You scream as loud as you can, louder than you have ever screamed in your life.

Instantly, other members of the crew appear on deck, some of them with lanterns. When they see the creature and its arms pulling at the railing, they scream too. There is chaos everywhere as sailors beat on the creature's arms with oars and with their fists. Some load their pistols and shoot at the monster in the water.

And amid the shouting and shooting, the huge eye—still without blinking—looks at you one more time. Then the beast pulls its thick arms and tentacles back down into the deep.

It is gone.

You collapse on the deck. The others surround you and ask what you saw. You tell them everything. The captain and several sailors nod. They know you're not making this up—because some of them have seen a similar monster on other voyages. A few have heard stories of men yanked off ships by huge tentacles, never to return.

They have heard stories of entire vessels pulled down to the ocean bottom, where the monster ate everyone on board.

You go to bed and try to forget what you have seen.

Months later, when you return home, you tell the story of the enormous creature with eyes as big as wheels and arms like vicious snakes. Back on land, though, no one believes you. It is a sailor's foolishness, they say, because sailors' imaginations work too hard after staring at miles of empty sea day after day after day. Besides, something that big would be seen all the time—maybe even from the land. One would have been caught by now.

No one believes your story, or those of other sailors. No one believes for hundreds and hundreds of years. No one believes until the day a team of oceanographers films a live beast with huge eyes and thrashing arms emerging from the sea.

Then there are *lots* of believers. The monster is real.

PART ONE

TALES OF THE

People have believed in monsters since the beginning of time.

For thousands of years, humans have been scared of many things they cannot see or understand. This was especially true in the centuries before electric lights were commonly used. Until then, most of the world stumbled through darkness each and every night, hearing the sounds of unseen wild animals, afraid to leave their homes after the sun went down. People stayed inside and lit fires to keep the unseen things away.

The world was an even scarier place for those people who traveled to places no one else had ever been before. Many of these men, women, and children went searching for new lands because they were looking for exciting adventures. Others had no choice and set out for uncharted lands in order to find better places to live, or to do business with other nations, or to bring back fish and timber and gold. Sometimes people, such as the Moors, who lived in eighth-century Spain and Portugal, and the Puritans, who lived in seventeenth-century England, were forced to flee their homes because of war or persecution by their enemies.

In many of these cases, that meant taking to the sea and confronting the unknown.

In every corner of the world, sailors loaded their boats and set off on long journeys. As far back as 1200 B.C., the ancient Greeks, Phoenicians, and Egyptians sailed the Mediterranean and built seaports so that they could trade goods with one another. At the same time, on the other side of the globe, the Polynesians sailed and paddled their way across thousands of miles of the Pacific Ocean to fish and barter with their island neighbors. Later on, in the ninth century, the fabled Vikings of Scandinavia took to the stormy North Atlantic in longships, seeking new lands to conquer, farm, and colonize.

MAPPING THE WORLD

These nations established regular sailing routes—usually the fastest and safest course between two points. Sailors charted their paths by the sun and the stars. As more and more ships set out to sea, these sailors needed more precise guides to get them from one place to another. Mapmakers, known as cartographers, were hired to draw detailed maps of the sailing routes. These maps showed the location of dry land and waterways, and oftentimes included descriptions of the tribes, animals, and plants that were located in distant lands.

At first, cartographers relied on descriptions from ship captains and crew members to create the maps. As ships sailed farther and more frequently out into uncharted waters, the cartographers went with the ships, mapping coastlines and identifying islands, reefs, and rough seas.

Image of ships at sea, by the Belgian artist Jan van der Straet from the late 1500s.

Typus Orbis Universalis. One of the earliest maps to show both the Old and New Worlds, this was drawn by the German cartographer Sebastian Münster (1488–1552) and published in 1550.

This is the first large-scale map of any European region, drawn by Olaus Magnus (1490–1557) of Sweden in 1539.

As trade between countries separated by water intensified in the 1400s, cartography became incredibly important. The more accurate the maps, the better the chances that the ships, sailors, and precious cargo would arrive at their destinations safely. Cartography was important for another reason: those countries that had knowledge about new lands and the best way to get there could use that information to dominate and even control the trade routes. Such domination would bring them more business, and more wealth, which would help them become richer and more powerful nations.

But there were many unexplored regions of the world, and cartographers were forced to leave those areas blank on their maps. Something was out there—maybe—but they didn't know exactly what. Like other people, the mapmakers heard from sailors that these faraway places were inhabited by mysterious beasts and sea serpents.

As a warning to those who used their maps, the cartographers adopted phrases to let sailors know that strange and even sinister creatures lurked just beyond the edge of the known world. On globes and maps they printed cryptic phrases—often written in Latin or local languages—to indicate the unknown or the spooky: "Here be dragons," "Here be lions," and "Here be dog-headed beings." Fanciful drawings frequently accompanied these words, showing animals—with huge teeth, horns, snakelike arms, and wings—peering out of the sea.

Anything beyond the boundaries of the map was considered dangerous. Sailors could look at a map and determine how far it was safe for them to go. But to anyone seeking to go into uncharted territory there was a warn-

with daggerlike teeth on the bottom of their heads (sperm whales). These were not animals that came close to the shore—they were out in the ocean, far from land and the safety it gave men—and only a few of the adventurers who described them had ever really seen them with their own eyes.

Yet even people who had never been in a boat were familiar with at least a few unusual sea creatures: small sharks, tiny squid, cuttlefish, octopuses, stingrays, seals, and other creatures were caught for food or for their skins. Many of them could be found in markets all over the world.

But sailors talked of monsters so bizarre and so huge that they could eat men in a single bite and destroy entire ships in the blink of an eye. They told stories of things that people on land could only imagine—or have nightmares about.

The most fearsome of all the mon-

ing that they all understood and took very seriously: "Here There Be Monsters."

There were certainly many strange creatures in the oceans, some more monstrous than others. Sailors encountered huge beasts climbing on rocks and roaring at the sky while their two-fanged heads dripped with seaweed (walruses), as well as giant flying bats soaring out of the water (manta rays). Fishermen were attacked in the water by fish with heads shaped like carpenter's tools (hammerhead and shovelhead sharks), and their ships had been rammed by black whales

sters in the ocean was said to be an enormous creature with many arms, huge eyes, a gaping mouth, and no body. Its arms were like gigantic snakes lined with thousands of sharp hooks and suckers that could grab on to a man and never let go. It was blood red, emitted a foul stench, and surrounded itself with black water. It looked like an octopus or a squid, only thousands of times bigger. The beast would rise up silently from the ocean deep and wrap its arms around a ship, trying to drag it under water. As it struggled, the monster grabbed sailors and tossed them into water, where they would soon become the monster's food.

De Montfort's drawing of a kraken destroying a ship during a storm.

No one had ever caught one of these creatures—they were too big, too strong, and too violent. But you could see the marks they made on the sides of boats, the sailors claimed. Even more frightening, they left their sucker marks on the bodies of huge whales that they attacked and fought to the death. The sailors saw these marks when they harpooned the whales out at sea. And since whales were the biggest and most powerful creatures in the ocean, the sailors could only wonder: *What kind of vicious beast would dare to fight a whale?*

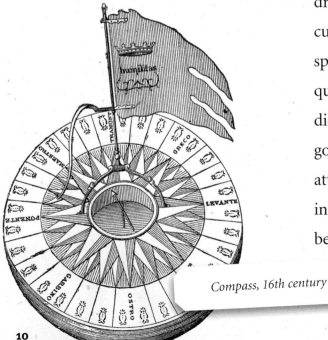

Compass, 16th century

THE BIRTH OF A LEGEND

It was easy for most people to dismiss these sea stories. After all, sailors spent months and even years at a time on their ships without coming home. The conditions onboard were filthy and hazardous by any standards. There were usually between thirty and fifty people—mostly men and boys—living and working onboard a vessel roughly the size of two school buses. Clothes were almost never changed and were washed even less: fresh water was used only for drinking and cooking. The most important food was hardtack, a dry tasteless cracker called a sea biscuit or molar breaker that wouldn't spoil on long trips. Food that spoiled quickly, like meat, fruit, and vegetables, didn't last long onboard. Meat would go rancid quickly, and sailors would attempt to make it last longer by keeping it soaked in salt water. There would be long days of no wind during which the ship would sit forlorn and unmoving under the blazing sun. Other times, icy wind and rain would lash the faces of those working on slippery decks, threatening to sweep them overboard during a storm. Illness was common, both from lack of fresh food and the churning motion of the waves. And almost every sailor experienced homesickness during the time spent away from friends and family.

These sailors' stories of dangerous beasts became the stuff of legend. In Greek mythology, a squidlike monster named Scylla lived under the water. She was described in one of the great works of literature, *The Odyssey*, written by a poet named Homer in the eighth century B.C. *The Odyssey* tells the story of a Greek soldier trying to sail home after a war. On his way, he must first pass Scylla. She is not a pleasant sight by any means:

Therein dwells Scylla, yelping terribly. . . . Verily she has twelve feet, all misshapen, six necks, exceeding long, and on each one an awful head, and therein three rows of teeth, thick and close, and full of black death. . . . By her no sailors yet may boast that they have fled unscathed in their ship, for with each head she carries off a man, snatching him from the dark-prowed ship . . .

Scylla's long necks would reach out and grab sailors, just like the arms of giant beasts that sailors in later centuries claimed to have seen. Those rows of teeth on the end of her necks were eerily similar to the rows of suckers with sharp teeth that lined the sea serpent's slithering arms.

The story of Scylla was part of ancient mythology, a scary segment in an entertaining story. It wasn't long, however, before creatures like Scylla began showing up in texts written by scholars and researchers. Pliny the Elder, a famous historian who compiled a book of history and science around A.D. 60, wrote of a sea creature with a head as big as several barrels and that had arms thirty feet long.

Classical image of Scylla found on ancient pottery.

In 1555, Olaus Magnus, a Swedish historian, described a fish with huge eyes surrounded by horns that looked like tree roots. This beast, according to Magnus, was so powerful that it was able to drown both ships and sailors.

Even as part of history books, the descriptions of these monsters were so bizarre that most people felt they were the creation of sailors who had been away from home just a little too long. But to the sailors out in the dark water, the monster that lived beneath the waves was real. It wasn't a myth; it wasn't a legend. It was deadly.

The stories piled up over the centuries. They were always the same: massive beasts with arms as thick as tree trunks, eyes bigger than plates, a horrendous odor, and a taste for destruction. Yet it wasn't until thousands of years after it had been described in *The Odyssey* that this monster received a proper name, one that would be used by sailors the world over.

It was named the kraken.

THE MONSTER IS GIVEN A NAME

The Swedish scientist Carl Linnaeus used the word *kraken* in his book *Systema Naturae,* printed in 1735. Linnaeus, who developed the way we name and classify living organisms (by assigning them to place in the hierarchy of life, from kingdom and phylum to genus and species), chose a German word for octopus, *krake,* to define all cephalopods, a type of sea creatures that includes octopuses, squid, and cuttlefish. Linnaeus used *krake* and its plural, *kraken,* merely as scientific terms for these animals; he wasn't describing huge sea serpents.

It was a few years later that another man put the name and the monster together for all time. That someone was Erik Ludwig Pontoppidan, a Danish-Norwegian priest and writer known as the Bishop of Bergen. Pontoppidan was the author of many books on subjects such as politics, economics, religion, and science. Today, he is best known for a book he wrote in 1752. Entitled *Forste forsog paa Norges naturlige historie (The Natural History of Norway),* it described the horrific kraken in detail.

When Pontoppidan began his book, his intention was to write a history of animals and plants in Norway. As part of his research, he interviewed sailors who told him about the kraken. There seemed to be many Norwegian sailors who had seen the great sea beast with demonic eyes and slithering arms, and lived in fear of it attacking their ships. Pontoppidan recounted the sto-

Drawing of Erik Pontoppidan

ries he was told of a gigantic creature that rose up out of the sea, as big as an island, with arms that spread out for a mile.

The Kraken is raising himself near the surface . . . they immediately leave off fishing, take their oars, and get away as fast as they can . . . he there shows himself sufficiently, though his whole body does not appear, which in all likelihood no human eye ever beheld . . . its back or upper part, which seems to be in appearance about an English mile and a half in circumference (some say more, but I chuse the least for greater certainty) looks at first like a number of small islands . . .

At last several bright points or horns appear, which grow thicker and thicker the higher they rise above the surface of the water, and sometimes they stand as high and large as the masts of middle sized vessels. It seems these are the creature's arms and, it is said, if they were to lay hold of the largest man-of-war [large sailing ships], they would pull it down to the bottom. After this monster has been on the surface of the water a short time, it begins slowly to sink again, and then the danger is as great as before, because the motion of this sinking causes such a swell in the sea, and such an eddy or whirlpool, that it draws down everything with it.

Pontoppidan succeeded in naming a sea creature that had been talked about for centuries. By calling the monster a kraken, he gave it a name that would be used by sailors for more than two hundred years—right up until today.

However, in relating a secondhand account of the kraken story in a history book—a book supposed to be based on fact and observation—Pontoppidan made a serious error. He also exaggerated the size of the kraken even more than sailors usually did. In fact, his description was too extreme: the idea that something was really as big as an island made people doubt that anything so huge could live anywhere on earth and not be seen more often. After all, they argued, it was the second half of the eighteenth century, and Europeans had explored most of the world. America had been colonized for more than 150 years. Australia, a continent on the opposite side of the world, had been discovered and mapped. Ships of all shapes and sizes were regularly sailing across every ocean and sea on the planet. Surely, the thinking went, there was nothing new that had yet to be discovered. With that in mind, many scholars sneered at Pontoppidan's kraken as nonsense.

Nonetheless, the stories about the kraken persisted—even as scientists and explorers learned more and more facts about the natural world. At a time when science was unlocking the mysteries of everything from electricity to chemistry, these fantastic kraken stories made their way into newspapers, magazines, and even textbooks. The most famous stories were told by a Frenchman named Pierre Denys de Montfort, who wrote several popular texts about squid and octopuses. De Montfort was a malacologist, a scientist who studies mollusks, a huge group of animals without backbones that includes cephalopods as wells as clams and snails.

In his 1802 book, *Histoire naturelle générale et particulière des mollusques* (*A General and Specific Natural History of Mollusks*), de Montfort included a drawing of a gigantic octopus-like creature grabbing the masts of a sailing ship. The beast is shown wrapping itself around the ship's hull and looks like it is ready to carry the entire ship down to the ocean floor. The malacologist claimed this was a depiction of a real event that occurred off the western coast of Africa. Allegedly, the sailors on the ship survived certain death only by hacking off the monster's arms with swords, knives, and axes. De Montfort called the beast the "colossal octopus."

De Montfort told other incredible stories. He reported that in 1782, during a sea battle between French and British warships, a colossal octopus had risen out of the ocean and attacked the fleets. The beast destroyed every ship it found . . . ten in all. De Montfort also related a story told to him by an American ship captain about a sperm whale his crew had caught. Sticking out of the whale's mouth, the captain claimed, was an arm that looked like it belonged to a squid or octopus. It had suckers running up and down its length, but it was no ordinary arm—it was forty-two feet long. That made it longer than a railroad car. Apparently the arm had been chewed off a giant octopus or squid by the whale, perhaps during a fight.

De Montfort based this drawing on a picture he found in Saint-Malo, Angola.

De Montfort's stories were identical to many of those that had been told before, but his descriptions were more precise and vivid. Unfortunately for him, the story of the sunken French and British warships turned out to be untrue—the ships arrived safely in Jamaica—and de Montfort's reputation was ruined. Some think he intended the story as a joke, but no one would do business with him or publish his writings after such a joke. With no one willing to hire him, it was said that he lost all of his money and eventually starved to death in 1820.

One of de Montfort's fantastic drawings depicting an attack by a "colossal octopus."

IF NOTHING ELSE, de Montfort's stories helped popularize the legend of the kraken throughout Europe and America. His writing is thought to have inspired many others, including Alfred Tennyson, a man who was to become one of the most important poets in the history of the English language. Tennyson wrote phrases that are often quoted in books and conversation, such as "'Tis better to have loved and lost than never to have loved at all."

In 1830, the twenty-one-year-old Tennyson wrote a fifteen-line sonnet about a many-armed monster that waited silently in the darkest depths of a watery world. It was called, simply, "The Kraken." Tennyson's sonnet described the kraken as something enormous and eerie, hiding itself in a world without light. He wrote that humans would never see the entire beast until the last day of the world, when it would rise up to show itself to both men and angels.

Over the course of his lifetime, Tennyson would write many poems—he became the poet laureate of England in 1850—but "The Kraken" was so popular, it immortalized the sea monster for all time.

Below the thunders of the upper deep;
Far, far beneath in the abysmal sea,
His ancient, dreamless, uninvaded sleep
The Kraken sleepeth: faintest sunlights flee
About his shadowy sides: above him swell
Huge sponges of millennial growth and height;
And far away into the sickly light,
From many a wondrous grot and secret cell
Unnumber'd and enormous polypi
Winnow with giant arms the slumbering green.
There hath he lain for ages, and will lie
Battening upon huge sea-worms in his sleep,
Until the latter fire shall heat the deep;
Then once by man and angels to be seen,
In roaring he shall rise and on the surface die.

Tennyson,
circa 1875.

At this point in history—the mid-1800s—people were readily discarding many superstitions in favor of scientific discovery. It was a time of great exploration and research. Governments sent scientific expeditions around the world to explore jungles, deserts, seas, and forests with the purpose of adding to mankind's understanding of the earth and the creatures on it.

Since no scientist had yet seen a real kraken, dead or alive, they began looking for evidence of the creature and investigated stories told by sailors and fishermen. They found that there were some very specific traits that were common to all the stories. In addition to its thick arms and massive eyes, the kraken was said to emit a vile odor that reeked of ammonia. And instead of a mouth in its cone-shaped head, it had a large birdlike beak that could tear apart its prey.

Coincidentally, strange beaks were regularly found in the stomachs of harpooned sperm whales. Too hard to be digested by the whale, the beaks were the only trace of some mysterious animal that the whales had eaten.

In addition to the beaks in their stomachs, some of these whales had circular scars on their tough skin—wounds that appeared to have been inflicted by strong suckers. It looked as if something had fought viciously against the giant mammals.

That raised even more questions for scientists. Sperm whales lived deeper in the ocean than any other whale. Could a creature that had both a beak and razorlike suckers be living at such depths?

According to some, it could only be the kraken.

Science continued to scoff at the notion that the kraken was real. But

Close-up photos of giant squid beaks.

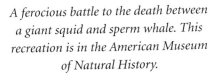

A ferocious battle to the death between a giant squid and sperm whale. This recreation is in the American Museum of Natural History.

many people, including quite a few scientists, changed their minds in the year 1870. That was the year when bodies of dead sea monsters mysteriously started showing up on beaches all over the world.

A piece of sperm whale skin with sucker scars. Look closely to see the tiny cuts made from the sharp blades that line the suckers.

PLATE 15.

PART TWO

WHAT WAS IMAGINED

Beginning in 1870, and frequently for the next ten years, huge tentacled beasts were found dead on the shores of countries around the world.

These carcasses were indeed monstrous, unlike anything that people on land had ever seen. No one knew why they appeared . . . and no one knew what had killed them. Newspapers worldwide reported on the strange phenomenon, and scientists rushed to collect samples of these beasts.

There were a few scientists who had seen creatures like this before. In fact, some of these scientists were sure that the animal washing up on beaches far and wide was not the mythical kraken but rather a strange species of squid . . . overgrown and possibly ferocious.

Several naturalists had already come to suspect that there might be a real creature that inspired the legend of the kraken. Many of the kraken's features— especially the long arms with rows of circular suckers, the bulbous head, the large eyes, and the beaklike mouth— were characteristics of three sea creatures: octopuses, squid, and cuttlefish.

The problem was that the vast majority of these creatures could be measured in inches; even the largest squid and octopus were rarely more than three or four feet long when fully stretched out. They were too little to cause panic and fear among strong men of the sea—and they certainly weren't big enough to destroy ships and drag them down to the ocean floor.

SCIENCE LOOKS FOR A SQUID

A Danish man named Japetus Steen-strup was convinced that the stories, pictures, and drawings of the kraken could be explained by the existence of an oversize squid. A giant squid, in fact. Since the 1850s, as a professor at the University of Copenhagen in Denmark, he had researched all the kraken sightings and stories he could find

MIGHT BE REAL

This picture of a giant squid washed up on a beach was printed in a Canadian newspaper in 1877.

from the previous two hundred years and put them together with what he knew of normal-size squid.

Steenstrup investigated claims by ship captains, fishermen, and others who had reported seeing squidlike beasts. He compiled a huge amount of information that, as far as he was concerned, supported the existence of a giant squid.

Like other scientists, he was faced with one very daunting task: finding evidence that there were giant squid. There had been reports of enormous squidlike bodies floating onto beaches in many places in northern Europe, primarily in Scandinavian countries. Bits and pieces of slimy arms with suckers had even found their way to local authorities. But they were literally bits and pieces. The problem was that by the time people found one of these giant dead things, its body had been eaten, chewed, nibbled, and all but swallowed up by everything from sharks and seagulls to local dogs. Little

was left that could be preserved. Even the outer skin was usually so torn up that it was hard to figure out what color the monster really was. And since it seemed to attract hungry seagulls and other animals, local people tended to cut up whatever was left and use it for bait and pet food.

That put researchers before Steenstrup in a difficult position. They had to rely on stories—not actual specimens—in their research. Good science required evidence.

Fortunately for Steenstrup, he had more than stories. He had a piece of evidence; a squid beak the size of a grapefruit (the beaks of smaller squid were tiny by comparison, from almost invisible to the size of grape). This beak had been retrieved from a monster found dead on a beach in Denmark. The rest of the creature had been destroyed before Steenstrup could see it, but he salvaged the beak. He kept it in a glass jar and showed it to his friends and associates.

Steenstrup believed that the beak, along with other body parts he had seen, were enough evidence to give a name to this rarely seen creature. He

Japetus Steenstrup, the man who named the giant squid Architeuthis dux.

named this animal *Architeuthis dux*. In Greek, *architeuthis* (pronounced arc-ih-tooth-iss) means "first or greatest squid," and *dux* means "king." By calling it architeuthis, Steenstrup was letting the scientific world know that he believed this creature was the king of all squid.

Despite his success in convincing the scientific community that the giant squid was real, there was still one thing missing from Steenstrup's research: the observation of a *living* architeuthis. It was one thing to listen to a story from a sailor who might have been scared out of his mind—or even obtain partial tentacles—it was quite another to have a scientist examine and study a giant squid up close.

The first real opportunity for science to get closer to architeuthis came in 1861 near the Canary Islands, off the coast of Africa. While patrolling in deep water, the French steamship *Alecton* came upon a floating beast with many arms and gigantic eyes.

Before the creature could dive away, the captain ordered his men shoot at it and try to grab it with ropes. They were able to loop some ropes around the body, but they eventually ripped through the beast, cutting it in half. What remained was a large part of the head section, which the captain sent back to France, along with his story of the ship's struggle with the beast. The details were then presented to the French Academy of Sciences, and they matched Steenstrup's description of a giant squid in almost every way.

So began a series of strange encounters with the giant squid, as if the monsters had suddenly decided to show themselves after centuries of hiding under the dark waves of the ocean.

THE MONSTER COMES TO THE SURFACE

From 1870 to 1880 there were dozens of sightings, and specimens, all over the world. They began in earnest in 1871, when a fishing boat off the eastern coast of Canada found the partially eaten body of a giant squid. The squid was taken back to shore and photographed. The picture was sent to Steenstrup, who now had photographic evidence of architeuthis. Then a full-length squid was found dead on the shore of Newfoundland in 1872; it was approximately fifty feet long from

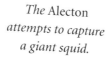

The Alecton *attempts to capture a giant squid.*

21

the tip of its tentacle to the end of its body. That is as long as a basketball court is wide.

The next time a giant squid was sighted, it sent shudders through those who heard about it. The event convinced many people that the giant squid and the kraken were really one and the same creature. It occurred in 1873, again in Newfoundland, only a year after the fifty-foot beast had been discovered.

Two fishermen were rowing their small boat in an area called Conception Bay. They saw something large spread out across the surface of the water, almost like pieces from a sunken ship. When they went to investigate, they saw that it was a dark red mass, like a huge mound of gelatin bobbing in the water. Just as they got close enough to touch it, the thing rose up and attacked them. According to reports, it whipped two tentacles up into the air and fiercely grabbed the boat, pulling it down into the water. The two men were sure to be dragged under and become the thing's next meal. As the boat tipped over, one of the men grabbed an ax and slashed at the tentacles, hacking at them until he cut them from the monster's body. The beast then slid back into the water, spewing a stream of black ink into the air as it disappeared.

Again, the story was like so many other kraken stories that had been told for hundreds of years. This time, though, there was one big difference. The two fishermen had saved the chopped-off tentacles to prove they were telling the truth.

They decided to take one of the tentacles, a nineteen-foot-long section, to a local reverend named Moses Harvey. In addition to being a minister, Reverend Harvey was a prolific writer. His articles had been published in newspapers all across Canada, the United States, and England. He was the perfect person to look at the tentacle because he had a special interest in history, science, and sea monsters.

After receiving the tentacle, Harvey wrote about the fishermen's struggle with the beast. He told of their heroism and bravery while being assaulted by what he called a "devil fish." Harvey

Drawing of a beached giant squid, circa 1875.

probably exaggerated a bit, but he had the tentacle to prove that the encounter had actually taken place.

Harvey's experience with giant squid didn't end there. Just a few weeks later, another squid—completely intact—was caught in a fishing net in Logy Bay, just a few miles from where the Conception Bay attack had occurred. The fishermen took the dead architeuthis to the reverend's home. He displayed it in his living room and draped it over a tub with the tentacles dragging on the floor. Stretched out, the squid was more than thirty feet long.

The reverend had the good fortune to be living in the right part of the world at the right time. During the 1870s, dozens of giant squid were seen off the coast of Canada, and many of them ended up dead on shore. But the Canadian sightings were only a fraction of the total number of architeuthis that were reported worldwide during a bizarre decade of strandings and sightings. In fact, giant squid were reported everywhere from the Indian Ocean to Ireland, and from Japan to Norway.

No one knew what was causing these great beasts to rise up and show themselves (an occurrence that Lord Tennyson obviously never expected). Scientists speculated that something was happening deep in the ocean; perhaps the giant squid's food supply was moving closer to the surface, or perhaps changes in the water temperature were forcing the giant squid to find more comfortable places to live . . . places that brought them perilously close to shore.

Whatever it was, the giant squid had now shown itself to be a real sea creature. The reality of its existence spurred more interest and

The giant squid on display in Rev. Moses Harvey's home.

excitement in the scientific community, not to mention in the imaginations of writers and artists around the world.

Harvey's writing and collection quickly earned him a reputation as a man who knew a great deal about giant squid. More and more fishermen brought him squid arms, suckers, and other bits that they caught or found. With all his expertise, however, Harvey knew that he wasn't qualified to study the giant squid at a scientific level. He decided to send his specimens to Professor Addison Verrill, a zoologist at Yale University in Connecticut.

Verrill had become Yale's first professor of zoology at age twenty-five. Known as a man who worked hard and slept very little, he ultimately wrote papers about and described more than a thousand new species of animals. Foremost among them was the giant squid. As a respected zoologist at a respected university, Verrill received squid specimens from all over the world to study. He created a collection of giant squid pieces and cataloged many of the sightings that occurred over the "sighting and stranding decade." This included a report from Reverend Harvey of a sixty-foot giant squid that had been captured in a little place called Thimble Trickle in Canada. Much to the dismay of scientists everywhere, the fishermen who measured the squid—still believed to have been the biggest ever seen—promptly decided to cut it up for bait.

Verrill became the premier expert on giant squid—although he, like every other researcher in the world, had never seen a live one. Based on his research, however, Verrill designed the first life-size model of a giant squid. It was forty feet long and made of papier-mâché. He put it on display in Yale's Peabody Museum.

Verrill believed that everyone should know about creatures such as architeuthis, not just scientists and scholars. He lectured regularly on his work, prompting the *New York Times* to run a story in 1880 entitled "Monsters of the Ocean," about the professor's research.

Addison Verrill

The newspaper called Verrill's work "one of startling interest."

With so many squid appearing on the coastlines of the world, it seemed as if science was getting all the specimens it could handle. But what scientists really wanted was to find a live squid, one that could be observed in its natural habitat. That, or perhaps a fisherman could catch a live one and keep it long enough for it to be studied.

Then, as suddenly as it began, the tide of giant squid and the regular sightings of them stopped. Architeuthis simply disappeared. It was as if the giant squid had decided once again to hide itself after ten years of appearing to people all over the world.

Stranger still was that the phenomenon of sightings and strandings would happen again exactly ninety years later.

FROM FACT BACK TO FICTION

As the nineteenth century drew to a close, the kraken had become a part of the scientific world, with a new name—architeuthis—and a new identity—the giant squid. But much of the information about the giant squid was shared between researchers, scientists, and university professors. The public wasn't aware of all the things being written in scientific papers or being discussed at university lectures. Outside of articles written by men such as Reverend Harvey and lectures given by Professor Verrill, there was not a lot of factual information that everyday people could find about the giant squid.

Instead, the giant squid was mythologized in books that were available to the public. Some of those books were so popular and sensational that the giant squid remained as frightening as it had been when it was the legendary kraken. Maybe even *more* frightening.

The first novelist to describe the giant squid was Herman Melville. Melville had sailed extensively throughout his life, seeking adventure and new experiences on ships that traveled across both the Atlantic and Pacific oceans. He described some of those adventures in *Moby Dick,* his book about the hunt for a menacing white sperm whale. *Moby Dick* was published in 1851, just as the first researchers were revealing that the kraken was most probably a type of giant squid. Melville wrote an entire chapter in *Moby Dick* describing the shocked reaction of sailors who saw a huge squid rise out of the ocean.

The sheer size of the floating beast in *Moby Dick* was enough to scare the sailors, even though they correctly identified it as a squid. But Melville's squid did no harm to the ship or its crew; it showed itself and then sank back into the water.

The crew in Jules Verne's popular novel *Twenty Thousand Leagues Under the Sea* was not so lucky. Verne's story, written in 1870, recounts the adventures of a submarine called the *Nautilus*, piloted by the mysterious Captain Nemo.

HERMAN MELVILLE, 1851
EXCERPT FROM CHAPTER 59, "SQUID"

Almost forgetting for the moment all thoughts of Moby Dick, we now gazed at the most wondrous phenomenon which the secret seas have hitherto revealed to mankind. A vast pulpy mass, furlongs in length and breadth, of a glancing cream-color, lay floating on the water, innumerable long arms radiating from its centre, and curling and twisting like a nest of anacondas, as if blindly to clutch at any hapless object within reach. No perceptible face or front did it have; no conceivable token of either sensation or instinct; but undulated there on the billows, an unearthly, formless, chance-like apparition of life. As with a low sucking sound it slowly disappeared again, Starbuck still gazing at the agitated waters where it had sunk, with a wild voice exclaimed: "Almost rather had I seen Moby Dick and fought him, than to have seen thee, thou white ghost!"

"What was it, Sir?" said Flask. "The great live squid, which they say, few whale-ships ever beheld, and returned to their ports to tell of it." But Ahab said nothing; turning his boat, he sailed back to the vessel; the rest as silently following. Whatever superstitions the sperm whalemen in general have connected with the sight of this object, certain it is, that a glimpse of it being so very unusual, that circumstance has gone far to invest it with portentousness. So rarely is it beheld, that though one and all of them declare it to be the largest animated thing in the ocean, yet very few of them have any but the most vague ideas concerning its true nature and form. . . . They fancy that the monster to which these arms belonged ordinarily clings by them to the bed of the ocean; and that the sperm whale, unlike other species, is supplied with teeth in order to attack and tear it. There seems some ground to imagine that the great Kraken of Bishop Pontoppodan may ultimately resolve itself into Squid.

While exploring the oceans of the world, the *Nautilus* encounters a giant squid, and it is not a happy meeting.

Verne's description has many similarities with the story of the French steamer *Alecton*, which had encountered the giant squid off the coast of Africa just nine years earlier. Verne actually mentions the *Alecton* earlier in his book, and it is likely he based his squid battle on what he had heard about the *Alecton*.

Even though the first samples of architeuthis had made their way to scientists' labs by the time *Twenty Thousand Leagues Under the Sea* was published, Verne described the giant squid as an eerie underwater beast every bit as terrifying as the legendary kraken. The popularity of his novel (much like the book *Jaws* a hundred years later) created fear in people who understood almost nothing about this undersea creature. For all they knew, it was a bloodthirsty, man-eating monster.

Outside of books, the giant squid kept itself hidden from view on all but a few occasions. Things were fairly quiet after all the sightings from 1870 to 1880. Dead squid were occasionally discovered on beaches or in fishermen's nets, but there were fewer and fewer of them. There was one significant sighting: the first giant squid found in the United States showed up in Massachusetts in 1909, floating off the coast of Cape Cod. Sailors onboard a boat named *Annie Perry* tried to pull it out of the water, but it separated into pieces. They did save a seven-foot-long tentacle, which was described as "perfectly fresh" by the captain.

Because of the earlier sighting and strandings, as well as the scientific recognition of *Architeuthis dux*, sailors in the early 1900s knew that the monster in the water was a giant squid. The Yale Museum had a life-size model of what it looked like, articles had been written, pictures had been taken, and specimens were being studied. And, in 1911, the great escape artist Harry Houdini performed a show in which he was chained up inside a "large sea monster" . . . most likely the carcass of a giant squid.

For all intents and purposes, the question of whether the kraken existed had been solved.

That is, until 1925. Two arms taken out of the stomach of a sperm whale caught near Antarctica that year were found to be much larger and more lethally armed than those of architeuthis. A British zoologist named Guy Robson determined that these arms were from a species that could be much larger than architeuthis. Based on just these two arms, he named the creature *Mesonychoteuthis hamiltoni* (pronounced mizz-on-a-kah-too-thiss hamil-tone-eye), and it would one day come to be known as the colossal squid. *Mesonychoteuthis* means "middle claw squid." But most scientists quickly forgot about this squid because no other evidence of it was found—until half a century later.

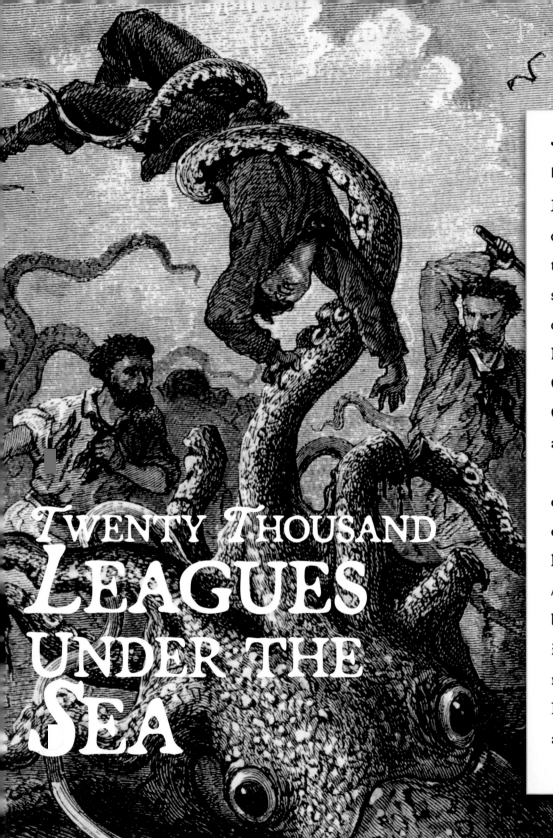

Twenty Thousand Leagues under the Sea

JULES VERNE, 1870

EXCERPT FROM CHAPTER 18, "THE POULPE"

Immediately one of these arms slid like a serpent down the opening, and twenty others were above. With one blow of the axe, Captain Nemo cut this formidable tentacle, that slid wriggling down the ladder. Just as we were pressing one on the other to reach the platform, two other arms, lashing the air, came down on the seaman placed before Captain Nemo, and lifted him up with irresistible power. Captain Nemo uttered a cry, and rushed out. We hurried after him.

What a scene! The unhappy man, seized by the tentacle, and fixed to the suckers, was balanced in the air at the caprice of this enormous trunk. He rattled in his throat, he was stifled, he cried, "Help! help!" These words, *spoken in French*, startled me! I had a fellow-countryman on board, perhaps several! That heartrending cry! I shall hear it all my life. The unfortunate man was lost. Who could rescue him from that powerful pressure? However, Captain Nemo had rushed to the poulp, and with one blow of the axe had cut through one arm. His lieutenant struggled furiously against other monsters that crept on the flanks of the *Nautilus*. The crew fought with their axes. The Canadian, Conseil, and I, buried our weapons in the fleshy masses; a strong smell of musk penetrated the atmosphere. It was horrible!

For one instant, I thought the unhappy man, entangled with the poulp, would be torn from its powerful suction. Seven of the eight arms had been cut off. One only wriggled in the air, brandishing the victim like a feather. But just as Captain Nemo and his lieutenant threw themselves on it, the animal ejected a stream of black liquid. We were blinded with it. When the cloud dispersed, the cuttle-fish had disappeared, and my unfortunate countryman with it. Ten or twelve poulps now invaded the platform and sides of the *Nautilus*. We rolled pell-mell into the nest of serpents that wriggled on the platform in the waves of blood and ink. It seemed as though these slimy tentacles sprang up like the hydra's heads. Ned Land's harpoon, at each stroke, was plunged into the staring eyes of the cuttle-fish. But my bold companion was suddenly overturned by the tentacles of a monster he had not been able to avoid.

Illustrations from the original version of Jules Verne's Twenty Thousand Leagues Under the Sea.

SECRETS FROM THE BELLY OF THE WHALE

Finding squid arms in a sperm whale may sound strange, but it was not unusual. One of the greatest sources of architeuthis specimens (as well as the only specimen of the colossal squid) was from sperm whales. For centuries, sperm whales were hunted for their meat and their spermaceti, a waxy compound in their heads that helps the whales adjust to changes in water pressure. This spermaceti was valued by merchants for its use as a lamp oil and a lubricant for gears in machines.

Sperm whales also produce an unusual substance called ambergris. This substance is excreted by sperm whales, possibly as vomit, and has long been used as an important ingredient in perfumes. Some scientists believe that ambergris is created in the whale's stomach in response to irritation caused by sharp giant squid beaks. The beaks are made of a substance called chitin, which is so hard that the whale's stomach acid can't dissolve it. Instead, it coats the beaks with ambergris, making them easier to pass. Because of its value in making perfume, ambergris is worth an incredible amount of money. (In 2006, a woman in New York found a four-pound chunk that was estimated to be worth $18,000.) It is often found floating in the water or sitting on beaches, but it can also be retrieved from dead whales.

When sperm whales were caught and cut up by whalers, the beaks, arms, tentacles, and various bits of giant squid were found undigested in the stomachs of the whales. Some parts of the squid, like the beak, wouldn't dissolve inside the whales.

During the nineteenth and twentieth centuries, however, the number of whales around the world decreased sharply due to hunting. This led many countries to ban whaling, including the hunting of sperm whales. While this was good for the whales, it did mean that one source of giant squid specimens was no longer available.

Zoologists wanted to learn more about the giant squid. There wasn't much more they could do, however, since whaling had stopped and giant squid weren't showing up on local beaches. And more than anything, these scientists wanted to find a live giant squid. But no one knew where to look for them.

In the 1950s, an American marine biologist named Frederick Aldrich wondered where all the giant squid could be. He decided to begin his search by studying the widespread appearance of architeuthis during the 1870s. By investigating weather patterns and ocean currents from the time, he came to believe that there were cold water currents that swept the giant squid up from the icy depths of the ocean, bringing the giant squid closer to the surface, and closer to shore. According to Aldrich, these currents would affect the squid every ninety years. That meant, according his calculations, that there should be more giant

A sperm whale dives down to the depths.

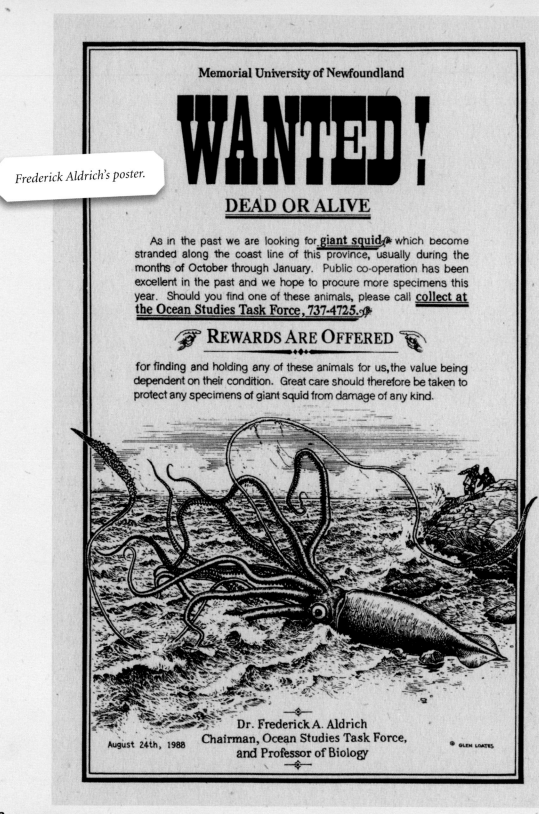

Frederick Aldrich's poster.

squid showing up in the 1960s.

He was right.

In the 1960s, the squid showed up almost as frequently as it had ninety years before. But this time, more of the squid were found in the Southern Hemisphere in New Zealand than in the dark and frigid waters of the North Atlantic Ocean. For some unknown reason, they were appearing half a world away from where most of them had been a century earlier.

There were still lots of giant squid to be found in every ocean, including the North Atlantic. During this time, Aldrich wanted to make sure he got new specimens for study. He and his students at Memorial University in Newfoundland put up signs around the eastern coast of Canada with the words WANTED DEAD OR ALIVE: A GIANT SQUID. Though no one brought him a live squid, two men who were transporting wood across a Canadian bay found a dead giant squid floating near their boat. They sent it to Aldrich, who took it to an airport to weigh it on a baggage scale. The squid weighed 331 pounds and was thirty feet long, making it the biggest specimen ever studied up to that point. Aldrich told a newspaper reporter that the suckers on this beast were two and a half inches in diameter. While that was impressive, Aldrich said, "I've seen whales with sucker scars twelve inches in diameter. Somewhere down there are giant squid 150 feet long."

During his career, Aldrich came upon fifteen specimens of the giant squid, but he never saw a live one. He knew that studies of the giant squid would not be complete unless it was studied alive—or at least seen in its natural habitat. He made it his mission to find one.

Aldrich became the first marine biologist to put together a plan to actively seek out and find architeuthis. In his determination to get a glimpse

of the animal, Aldrich raised enough money to launch a single underwater search. For half a day, he sat in a submersible one thousand feet below the ocean surface off the coast of Canada, waiting, watching, and hoping. Aldrich saw many types of marine life that day, but the giant squid was not one of them. Sadly, he died two years later before he could begin another expedition. But he left behind a desire on the part of others to continue his work: to find the giant squid alive.

It wasn't until the end of the twentieth century that the next major search for a live giant squid took place, involving researchers, submarines, film crews, and

museums from all over the world. The goal was to find and photograph a living architeuthis, one of the most astonishing creatures anywhere on the planet.

Although researchers had never examined a live giant squid, they had already learned an amazing amount about this most mysterious of creatures. And that knowledge would help them in their deep-sea search for the elusive architeuthis.

PART THREE

A REAL-LIFE

Scientists had learned a great deal about architeuthis from the carcasses and bits of tentacles that had been collected over the course of a century.

The most significant thing was that the giant squid was a head-foot.

Actually, all squid are head-foots. Their scientific name is the Greek word *cephalopod* (*cephalo* for "head" and *pod* for "foot"). Squid were originally called this because they seemed to have only two obvious parts: the head and the feet, with no body in between. The feet, of course, turned out to be the tentacles and arms.

There is probably no other animal form on earth that seems so different from humans than the cephalopod. Even snakes, which have no limbs, have a face people can relate to: eyes, mouth, and nose all on the front of a head. Insects, despite their small size, seem normal to us because their head and feet and mouth and eyes are all in the right places. Even their limbs stick out from their bodies in expected ways.

But cephalopods are an entirely different story. Many of them have huge eyes on a bulbous head, with no visible nose or mouth. Their snakelike arms are covered with suckers, and they twist and turn in ways that no mammalian arms or legs ever could. Their mouths are hidden deep in these arms, but they are not normal-looking mouths. They are hard and beaklike, as if they came from a giant bird. Add to that their underwater habitat, and it doesn't get much creepier than a cephalopod.

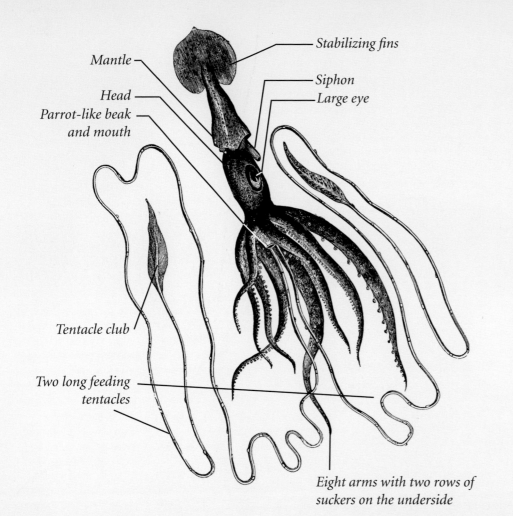

Mantle

Head

Parrot-like beak
and mouth

Stabilizing fins

Siphon

Large eye

Tentacle club

Two long feeding
tentacles

Eight arms with two rows of
suckers on the underside

like connections between its nerves, called axons, are very similar to those in humans and can be seen with the naked eye. These squid axons are hundreds of times thicker than human axons, and scientists have used them to help understand how signals travel from the human brain to other parts of the body.

The giant squid has all of these squid features in a monster-size package . . . and quite a bit more. It is thought that they can grow from less than one inch at birth to more than twenty feet just two years later. But we know so little about them that we're not exactly sure how long they live or what they die from.

Architeuthis is made up of several distinct sections. The first part is the mantle, which is the giant squid's body. On the largest giant squid, this can be up to seven feet long (or tall, depending on how you're looking at the squid). Running partway down each side of the mantle are two fins, which help the squid steer through the water.

What you would naturally think of as being the tip of the squid's head is really its tail, at the end of the mantle. The head is tucked down at the bottom of the mantle near the tentacles. Here is where the giant squid's two huge eyes and its incredibly strange mouth are. The eyes of the giant squid range in size from a few inches, like small plates, to a foot or so across, each as big as a pizza. The only creature in the animal kingdom with eyes bigger than a giant squid is the colossal squid. The eyes of mesonychoteuthis can each be more than a foot wide and resemble a beach ball.

This image of a squid eye is eight inches across. A real colossal squid's eye can be as big as thirteen inches across.

The mouth, as you and ancient sailors know by now, is similar to the beak of a vulture or a parrot, and protrudes from the underside of the head. The beak is made of chitin, a hard bony substance that enables the giant squid to tear its prey to pieces. Chitin is the same substance that the shells of crabs and lobsters are made of.

Though the beak looks odd and out of place, the inside of the giant squid mouth is like something from a horror movie. Architeuthis has a tongue-like muscle covered with rows of tiny, sharp blades, also made of chitin. This is called the radula, and it is used to slice up prey once the arms insert the prey into the squid's mouth. Think of the radula as a tongue with the teeth built right into it. The radula also helps the mouth push food down into the stomach, which is located at the far end of the mantle.

Between the head and the mantle is a funnel, which the squid uses to move through the water. Other creatures use their fins, flippers, or feet to swim through the water, but the giant squid's arms and tentacles do not help it swim. Instead, the funnel squirts water out of the squid's body, propelling it.

Think of the giant squid's mantle as a gigantic balloon. Instead of blowing up the balloon with air, the squid fills it up with water by sucking it in through an opening near the funnel. Water fills up the balloon section, which is called the mantle cavity. When the cavity is full of water, the squid seals the opening, just as you would with a balloon. Then it forces the water out through its funnel.

This is a close-up photo of a radula, showing the teethlike blades on the tongue. This particular radula belongs to a squid known as Onkyia indica, *and the picture was taken using a scanning electron microscope.*

The colossal squid's beak protruding from its mouth.

What happens is exactly what happens when you let go of a balloon. The air rushes out, propelling the balloon in the opposite direction. As the giant squid squirts the water out of its funnel, it shoots its whole body in the opposite direction. Its tail—the tip of the mantle—guides it the way it wants to go. The arms and tentacles trail behind as the giant squid jets quickly through the water.

Most people would agree that the arms and the tentacles are the scariest part of the giant squid because they are unlike anything we see on mammals, birds, or even fish. The giant squid has eight arms, just like an octopus and a cuttlefish. The arms extend down from around the mouth, away from the head. These are used for holding food once it is caught and guiding the food into the mouth. Unlike the octopus, the giant squid never uses its arms to pull it across the ground or over rocks and coral.

The giant squid has two tentacles, which are much longer than its arms. These are used for grabbing its food. All squid and cuttlefish have tentacles, but the octopus does not; many people mistakenly refer to octopus arms as tentacles.

The tentacles are the longest part of the squid. Throughout history, giant squid have been measured from the top of the mantle to the tip of the tentacle. Modern teuthologists—the scientists who study squid—think this is the wrong way to figure out how long a giant squid really is. Because the tentacles of a dead specimen can be stretched—much like rubber bands—they might be pulled farther than they ever were while the squid was alive. This may be why some giant squid specimens have been measured at sixty feet. Today, scientists usually measure just the length of the mantle in order

The author showing the suckers on an architeuthis tentacle.

to give more accurate comparisons between specimens.

It is the giant squid's suckers that make this cephalopod the creature of nightmares. Like other cephalopods, the giant squid has rows and rows of suckers running up and down the length of its arms and tentacles. These suckers help the arms latch on to prey and hold it tightly. They also help cephalopods determine the hardness or softness of prey, almost like the sensitive tips of your fingers.

The suckers of an octopus are smooth and round. The suckers of the giant squid, however, are far different. They have small weapons built into them. The circumference of each sucker is ringed with sharp teeth, almost like the blades of a circular saw. As the giant squid grabs on to its prey, not only do these sucker rings squish themselves onto the skin of the prey, but their tiny blades cut into the prey's skin and grab on. These teeth line

the suckers on both the arms and the tentacles.

The giant squid's tentacles flatten out at their tips, forming what are called tentacle clubs. It is thought that these clubs float in the water and clap on to passing prey like big catcher's mitts. Once these clubs latch on to something, the squid can then tighten its grasp by locking the suckers on the shafts of its two tentacles together, almost like two Velcro strips pressed together.

The tentacles lock the prey, usually fish, in a stranglehold long enough for the squid to pull its body up and wrap around the fish. Then its arms hold the food still while the beak and radula eat it up. Giant squid eat fish of all sizes as well as smaller squid, although they will eat almost anything that comes nearby, including other giant squid.

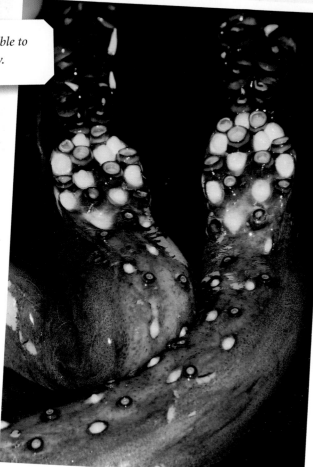

Tentacle clubs are able to latch on to prey.

LIFE IN DARKNESS

The giant squid hunts in a world of utter darkness. It lives so far beneath the surface of the ocean that sunlight cannot penetrate to its home . . . and the normal water temperature is only a few degrees above freezing. At two thousand feet down—where scientists believe the giant squid lives—the ocean is darker merge only to about fifteen hundred feet below the surface without getting crushed by the weight of the water.

Giant squid move easily through water even deeper than this—some experts think they might be able to descend a mile or more below the surface. They don't experience the pressure that would squash a submarine because their bodies have no air inside them. Also, the water that flows through them makes their body equal to the pressure from the surrounding water.

Since there is no air or gas in the giant squid, scientists wondered for years how it could float to the surface of the ocean and then drop back down to where the pressure would crush a car instantly. In some sightings, the giant squid appeared to float motionless on the surface, leading to the belief that changes in water pressure have severely injured the creatures—especially younger ones—as they rise up from the depths.

A group of sperm whales swimming just below the ocean's surface.

than outer space. The only light comes from small creatures that glow in the dark. The bodies of these creatures are filled with bioluminescent chemicals, which means that they can create a cold light that causes them to glow. This light is used to either attract prey or to scare off predators. It is thought that the giant squid's eyes are so big in order to see even the tiniest specks of light in total darkness.

At depths of a thousand feet or more below the surface, the pressure of the water is equal to several thousand pounds per square inch. This is about the weight of an entire dump truck squeezed into a space the size of a postage stamp. Such pressure would crush animals that live on land into nothingness. Even naval submarines, with their thick metal hulls, can sub-

That does not explain those giant squid that have appeared at the top of the water and then dived back down, seemingly unaffected by the changes in pressure. In many fish, there is a sac or bladder filled with gas (such as oxygen) that helps them rise and descend to different depths. Adding more oxygen helps the fish rise; expelling it helps them sink. But the giant squid has no air sac.

It turns out that architeuthis is able to rise and fall thanks to an unusual chemical: ammonia.

Ammonia is a highly toxic chemical with a very distinct and unpleasant odor. It is used as a cleaning fluid, as fuel, as fertilizer, and it is also one of the components of urine. The giant squid's body is saturated with ammonia, which it stores up from its own waste. Ammonia is lighter than seawater, so it will naturally rise up through the ocean (in much the same way that oil separates and rises through water). Depending on what the squid wants to do, it adjusts the amount of ammonia in its body. If it wants to be buoyant, meaning that it wants to rise, it holds the ammonia in. If it decides to descend, it spews ammonia out.

The ammonia accounts for the stench that sailors claimed to have smelled emanating from the kraken. It also makes the giant squid particularly distasteful. Many species of squid are quite delicious—and are served as calamari at restaurants—but the ammonia in their bodies makes the giant squid too foul to eat.

However, there is one animal that thinks the giant squid is quite a treat: the sperm whale. When giant squid remains were first discovered in the stomachs of sperm whales, it was thought that the squid might have attacked the whales with the intent of eating them. Scientists now believe that whales hunt the squid, not the other way around. Any "fights to the finish" between these two ocean giants probably resulted from the giant squid defending itself from being eaten by the sperm whale. In fact, most researchers today believe that the giant squid is not nearly as aggressive and ferocious as the legend of the kraken has led us to believe.

We know that sperm whales eat a lot of giant squid, but we don't know how they catch the squid. When partially digested giant squid have been found in the stomachs of sperm whales, they are not always chewed up. This has led scientists to wonder how a sperm whale can grab a giant squid—armed with its lethal suckers, tentacles, and a beak—and swallow it whole without first having to kill it by chewing it. It would seem that the giant squid, which can jet quickly through the ocean, should be able to avoid capture by the sperm whale.

Making the whale's hunt more difficult, it must hold its breath to find the giant squid. The whale is a mammal, and it needs to breathe air. Sperm whales can stay under water for more than an hour on a single breath. That really isn't much time when you consider that it must dive down thousands of feet, find a giant squid in total darkness, grab it, eat it, and then shoot back up thousands of feet to the surface—all before it runs out of air.

Yet based on the number of beaks found in their stomachs, sperm whales do this hundreds if not thousands of a times a year. They find plenty of giant squid day in and day out. This is an incredible feat considering that, with all our technology, humans have still not been able to follow one single giant squid while it was under the water.

So how does the sperm whale find the giant squid, one of its favorite foods?

No one is quite sure, although there is one theory favored by many scientists. Sperm whales have a well-developed form of "biological radar" or echolocation, similar to that used by bats. They emit a series of clicking sounds from inside their huge head that bounce around the dark waters. When the sound waves hit something and bounce back to the whale, it is then able to locate the object in the dark. Some scientists believe that the size of the sperm whale allows it to emit sounds so powerful and intense that they actually can stun or even kill its prey. If such a sound were to knock out or kill a giant squid, it would help to explain how sperm whales can snag squid and swallow them without chasing them for hours or chewing them up.

That still leaves all those deep sucker scars on the sperm whales to wonder about. Certainly they are caused by giant squid fighting back against the sperm whale, which is the largest predatory mammal on earth. So sometimes the squid have to be awake. But since no human has ever seen these two creatures actually do battle, we can only imagine what happens. Perhaps the giant squid sees the sperm whale first and attempts to kill the whale before it can be eaten. Or perhaps the stunned squid is snagged by the whale but is able to respond before it is swallowed. Or maybe the squid lashes out at the whale to keep it away from its own food. Right now, we just don't know.

Adding to the mystery, many sperm whales have been found with scars that resemble cuts from a knife or a razor in and around the sucker scars. Since the giant squid has no daggerlike weaponry on its tentacles—it does have the round saw blades on its suckers—something else was making those cuts. Researchers were baffled as to what kind of creature could inflict such wounds.

It seemed there was the possibility that another animal, bigger and deadlier than the giant squid, was lurking down in depths. Maybe there was more than one beast that fit the description of the kraken . . .

Scientists got their answer in 1981. That year, off the coast of Antarctica, a Russian fishing vessel accidentally caught a large squid on lines that had been dropped more than 2,000 feet below the surface. When the fishermen pulled it up, the squid was obviously not architeuthis—its body was too big and it was a different shape. Upon examination, it proved to be *Mesonychoteuthis hamiltoni,* the same squid that had been identified by the unusual arms found in a sperm whale in 1925. That squid had been all but forgotten in the half-century since it was first discovered.

It was the first time in history that the body of *Mesonychoteuthis hamiltoni* had ever been seen. The squid was photographed and measured while it lay on the deck of the Russian trawler. It was thirteen feet long and not yet full grown. Researchers estimated that it might have grown to four times that size had it not been caught. The sailors did not keep any of the *Mesonychoteuthis hamiltoni* because there was no way to preserve it.

Twenty-two years later, in 2003, the first complete specimen of *Mesonychoteuthis hamiltoni* was caught off the coast of Antarctica and sent to a lab in New Zealand. It was the body of a female squid. Although not fully grown, it was twenty feet long.

Because of its size, researchers decided to give it a name that indicated it was indeed something bigger and perhaps deadlier than even the giant squid. They named it the colossal squid.

The mantle of the colossal squid is much larger than that of the giant squid, growing up to twelve feet in length. Its eyes are the biggest of any organism on our planet, and may each grow to be more than two feet wide. Its arms are shorter than those of architeuthis, but

The first photograph of a colossal squid, taken in 1981.

its tentacles are much more frightening. Like architeuthis, it has suckers ringed by small teeth that resemble saw blades on its arms and tentacles. But *Mesonychoteuthis hamiltoni* has something else that adds to its nightmarish appearance. Inside the suckers on the clubs of its tentacles are individual hooks—like small tiger claws—that stick out of the sucker. They can each swivel individually, like probing razors. They are sharp enough to dig deep into prey.

These flesh-tearing hooks explain the scars on the skin of sperm whales. From the looks of it, the colossal squid's body is structured to be more aggressive and more predatory than the giant squid's.

Dr. Steve O'Shea examines the knifelike hooks that stick out of the colossal squid's suckers.

Humans have been to the moon six times and retrieved more than two thousand rocks. The moon is 250,000 miles away from earth. Yet scientists have collected only about two dozen specimens of the colossal squid, a creature that lives less than one mile under the ocean. It is odd that we have more specimens from a place that is a quarter of a million miles away than we do of one of the biggest creatures on the earth, even though it lives right here in our oceans.

There is still so much science doesn't know about these monstrous cephalopods: how big giant and colossal squid get, how many of them there are, how fast and how far they can travel, how they reproduce, or how long they live. Even though the giant squid exists in every ocean (based on current evidence, the colossal squid appears to live only near Antarctica) and has been sighted on every continent, it has many secrets.

That is why scientists set out to find and film these huge squid, using every-thing from submarines to underwater cameras. Beginning in 1997 and continuing right up until today, there have been a number of expeditions hoping to find an architeuthis or mesonychoteuthis alive and in its own watery world.

It was a long time in coming, but after more than a thousand years, the giant squid and the colossal squid finally did show themselves to the entire world. Alive, and on camera.

Close-up of mesonychoteuthis hooks.

PART FOUR

THE MONSTER RISES

The myth of the kraken and the portrayal of the giant squid as a huge predator have been kept alive in front of movie cameras—and in the pages of books—for a long time.

In 1954, Walt Disney produced a movie version of *Twenty Thousand Leagues Under the Sea*. The film featured a harrowing scene of a giant squid grabbing on to Captain Nemo's *Nautilus* submarine and then fighting the crewmen on board. While the squid looked real enough—right down to the flailing tentacles and chomping beak—it was actually a large mechanical model built in a studio. In 1958, Ian Fleming had his master spy James Bond fight a giant squid in the novel *Dr. No*.

In 1991, Peter Benchley, the author of *Jaws*, wrote a book called *Beast*. It featured an angry architeuthis off the coast of Bermuda. The two stories were very similar: like the great white shark in *Jaws*, the giant squid terrorized a resort town by eating sailors and swimmers for lunch. And just like in real life, no amount of technology or weaponry could find the creature. In 1996, it was made into a TV movie called *The Beast*.

The kraken pulls a sailing ship into the ocean in a scene from Pirates of the Caribbean: Dead Man's Chest.

In the twenty-first century, Disney once again brought the giant squid to the movies—or at least the kraken version of the giant squid. In *Pirates of the Caribbean: Dead Man's Chest,* the kraken rises up to attack ships when it is summoned by Davy Jones. At the end of the movie, it swallows the hero, Captain Jack Sparrow, and takes him down to the ocean floor. In the next movie of the trilogy, *At World's End,* the kraken has spit Captain Jack out . . . and its gigantic form lies dead on a beach. As real as this kraken looked, it was created using computer animation.

Seeing the giant squid on movie screens was one thing. But filming a live architeuthis was still the dream of many zoologists. And since neither the giant squid nor the colossal squid were showing up any place where scientists could find them alive, the scientists had to go looking on their own.

Because both the giant and colossal squid live so deep in the ocean, getting down to their habitat would require very advanced equipment. It would be like mountain climbing in reverse. High-tech cameras, submersibles, ships, and a trained crew were needed—and they weren't free. That meant that a search

for these squid would be expensive. A single expedition could cost more than a million dollars. Raising the money and then preparing the mission would take many months, and that was before the scientists even got in the water. Then they would spend several more months looking for it.

The first major long-term expedition for the giant squid was led by a zoologist named Clyde Roper. As a teenager, Roper had worked on lobster boats in New Hampshire. He had heard all the legends of the giant squid time and time again. But as an adult, he wasn't interested in the myths; he wanted to find the real thing.

Roper looks like he could have been a crew member in *Moby Dick.* He has whiskers that frame his jaw and he speaks with the thick accent of a New England fisherman. Instead of life on a boat, however, he chose the life of a zoologist. Specifically, he is a marine biologist specializing in cephalopods, which is the definition of a teutholo-

Clyde Roper, sitting with the eyeball of a giant squid.

gist. His career took him to the Smithsonian Institution, where he became the museum's head of invertebrate zoology—the very department where squid of all types are studied. Roper immersed himself in the world of the giant squid, even tasting part of one to see if it would make good calamari (it wouldn't).

While he was at the Smithsonian, Roper inherited the informal title of the world's foremost expert on the giant squid. It was a title that had first been used to describe Japetus Steenstrup in Denmark. When Steenstrup retired, Addison Verrill at Yale became the leading authority on architeuthis. The next man to be hailed as the world's giant squid expert was Frederick Aldrich.

After Aldrich's death in 1991, Roper picked up where Aldrich had left off. In 1996, he decided to go looking for architeuthis on his own.

Roper began a series of expeditions that involved people from the United States, New Zealand, the United Kingdom, and Canada. These researchers had all examined giant squid specimens in their labs and had spent years learning all they could about the animal. If anyone would be able to find architeuthis, it seemed that they would be the ones. Plus, they had lots of support for their quest: money, supplies, and support came from partners ranging from National Geographic, the British Broadcasting Company (BBC), NASA, New Zealand's National Institute of Water and Atmospheric Research, and the Massachusetts Institute of Technology, to the Office of Naval Research, the Smithsonian, and the Discovery Channel.

For the first of Roper's three missions, he and his team traveled to the Azores, a group of islands in the Atlantic Ocean approximately midway between Canada and Portugal. There they followed sperm whales, knowing that the whales would be hunting the giant squid for food. Roper referred to the whales as "hound dogs" because the human explorers would use them to track the squid. They even attached a camera—known as a crittercam—to the back of a sperm whale and saw what the whale saw as it dove deep into the ocean in search of food. (The crittercam was also attached to a penguin for the filming of the movie *March of the Penguins*.)

Unfortunately, the crittercam on Roper's expedition was knocked loose by another sperm whale several hundred feet under water. Nonetheless, the team learned a great deal about sperm whales during the journey—and even filmed them sleeping while floating upright—yet they never found any sign of a live giant squid.

First Roper Expedition for Architeuthis

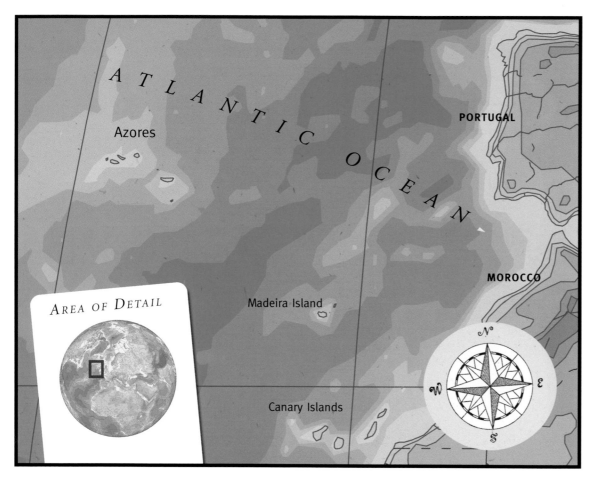

Not one to give up, Dr. Roper went back to search for architeuthis the following year. This time his team went to New Zealand, where local fisherman had recently hauled up the bodies of dead giant squid. There they explored a place known as Kaikoura Canyon, a deep oceanic trench off the eastern coast of the south island of New Zealand. This time, along with another crittercam, they sent a small unmanned submarine called the *Odyssey II* into the water (remember that the mythical Scylla had been described in Homer's *Odyssey*). Again, the team learned a great deal about the geology and biology of the giant squid's environment and encountered rarely seen creatures like the dogfish shark, but there was no sign of the giant squid itself.

Heading down into the water one more time in 1999, Roper and his team revisited Kaikoura Canyon. There's a saying that "the third time's a charm," and Roper was hoping this would be it.

But it wasn't. No amount of high-tech gear, computers, sonar, submarines, or expensive equipment was able to find either architeuthis or mesonychoteuthis. While the submersible Roper's team sent into the ocean set new records for how deep humans had gone into the waters around New Zealand (2,200 feet) and many species were seen for the first time, architeuthis was nowhere to be found. As Roper reported at the end of his trip, "The giant squid remains an elusive, though real, mystery of the deep."

Roper was named zoologist emeritus after retiring from his full-time position at the Smithsonian in 2002.

Like other teuthologists before him, Roper had become a well-respected and world-famous investigator of the giant squid. And like those before him, he had never seen a live giant squid.

Once again the mantle of "leading expert on the giant squid" was passed to another researcher. This time it was a young marine biologist named Steve O'Shea, a professor at the Auckland University of Technology. O'Shea had spent much of his career as a researcher at New Zealand's National Institute of Water and Atmospheric Research (NIWA) in Wellington. One day he was asked to study a giant squid found by a local fisherman, and at the site found himself bombarded by questions from news reporters. From that day forward, he became New Zealand's squid guy. He learned all he could about architeuthis and eventually participated in two of Clyde Roper's expeditions. O'Shea went on to lead two expeditions of his own in 2000 and 2001, which found the larva of a giant squid—tiny unhatched babies—off the coast of New Zealand. The larva can be identified as giant squid only by a microscope, and even then it takes a trained expert like O'Shea to be sure they are baby giant squid and not some other form of squid. Although none of the larva survived, O'Shea was committed to unraveling the tangle of mysteries that still surrounded the giant squid.

O'Shea was a man in the right place at the right time. Just as specimens

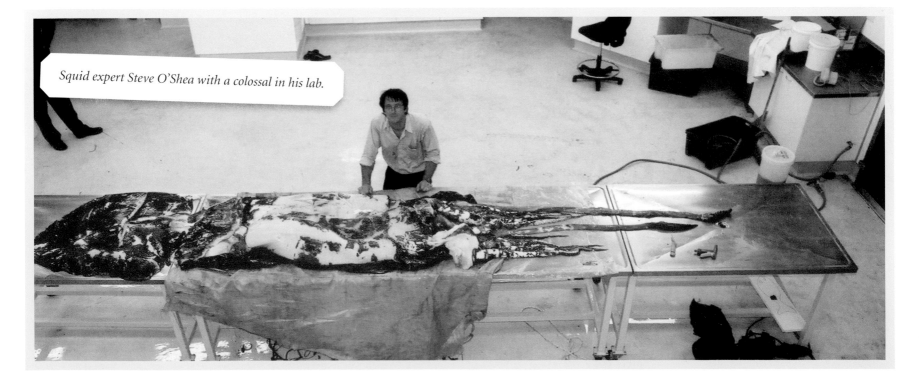

Squid expert Steve O'Shea with a colossal in his lab.

SECOND AND THIRD ROPER EXPEDITIONS FOR ARCHITEUTHIS

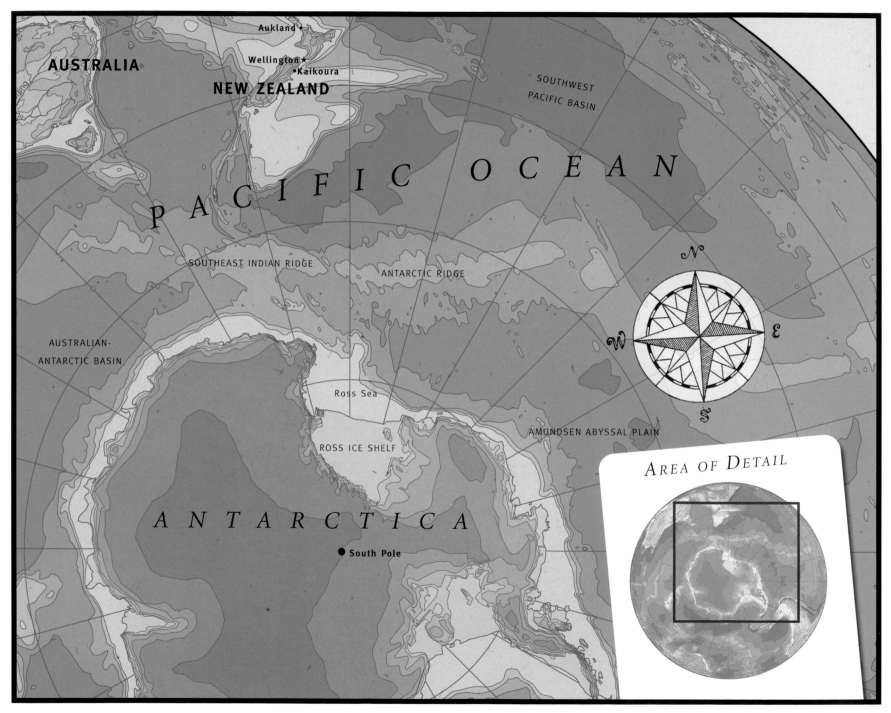

AUSTRALIA

Aukland

Wellington ★
• Kaikoura

NEW ZEALAND

SOUTHWEST
PACIFIC BASIN

PACIFIC OCEAN

SOUTHEAST INDIAN RIDGE

ANTARCTIC RIDGE

AUSTRALIAN-
ANTARCTIC BASIN

Ross Sea

ROSS ICE SHELF

AMUNDSEN ABYSSAL PLAIN

ANTARCTICA

● South Pole

AREA OF DETAIL

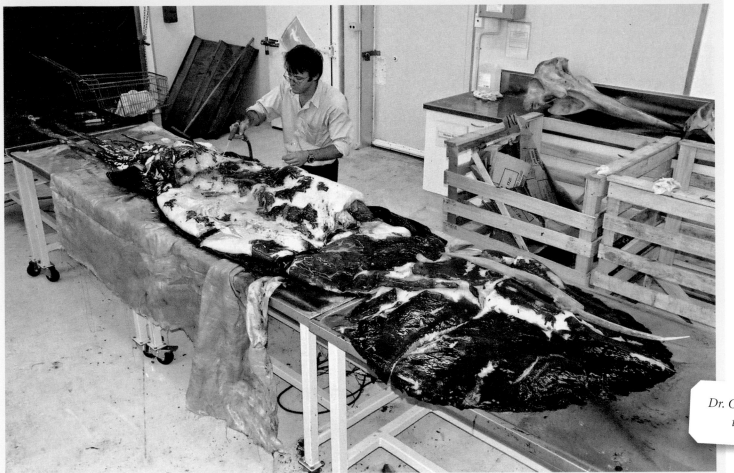

Dr. O'Shea begins studying the colossal squid.

had been sent to Yale University 130 years earlier, now the specimens were going to Auckland and Wellington—in part because many of them were getting hauled up by fishing boats around New Zealand and Antarctica and O'Shea's lab was the nearest place to send freshly caught giant squid. In the next few years he examined more than a hundred specimens. And then he received a specimen that no other researcher had ever examined before.

In February 2003, an intact female *Mesonychoteuthis hamiltoni* was found floating in the Ross Sea, an icy expanse of water tucked into Antarctica, at the bottom of the world. The fishing boat that came upon it brought the body to New Zealand, where O'Shea and his staff were able to examine the creature. It was the first opportunity that scien-

The gigantic eye of a colossal squid.

Researcher Kat Bolstad takes measurements of the colossal squid.

tists ever had of examining an intact mesonychoteuthis specimen.

It was O'Shea's group that named this creature the colossal squid. They did this for two reasons: first, so that this particular squid could have a common name that everyone could use and pronounce (even scientists admit that *Mesonychoteuthis hamiltoni* is difficult to say all the time), and second, to highlight that this squid was extremely big, more lethally armed, and very likely more aggressive and more powerful than the giant squid.

O'Shea's team determined that this particular colossal squid was a young female, perhaps only half grown. Still, it weighed more than three hundred pounds and was sixteen feet long. After examination, the squid was turned over to the Museum of New Zealand, Te Papa Tongarewa in Wellington, where it was displayed for several months before being stored in the museum's mollusk collection for safekeeping.

With all the specimens that kept showing up in New Zealand and in the North Atlantic, eager researchers continued to hope that the cold waters near Antarctica and the Arctic would eventually produce a living squid. They kept focusing their attention there.

It turned out that they should have been looking in Japan.

On September 30, 2004, a team of explorers from the National Science Museum of Japan dropped a line with a camera attached to it into the deep waters surrounding the Ogasawara Islands in the North Pacific Ocean. Japanese researchers had known for years that the this area was a feeding ground for sperm whales, and they knew that sperm whales liked to eat giant squid. Not only that, but fishing boats had occasionally snagged architeuthis around the islands. The researchers, led by a man

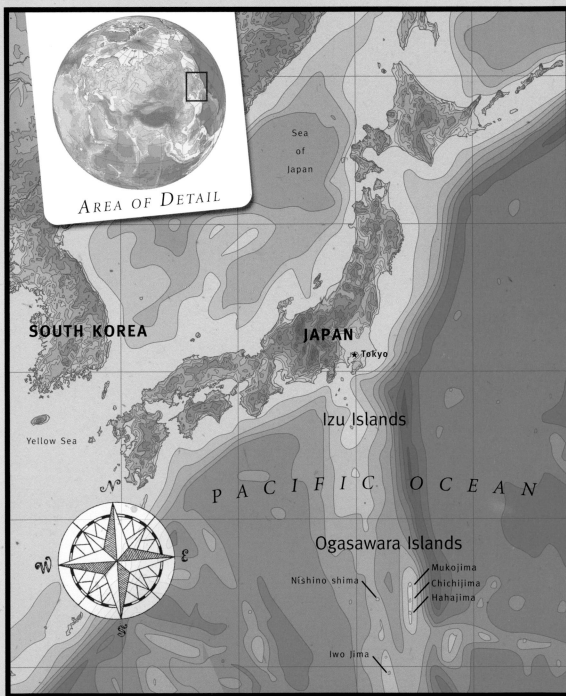

JAPAN

AREA OF DETAIL

Sea
of
Japan

SOUTH KOREA

JAPAN

★ Tokyo

Yellow Sea

Izu Islands

PACIFIC OCEAN

Ogasawara Islands

Mukojima
Níshino shima
Chichijima
Hahajima

Iwo Jima

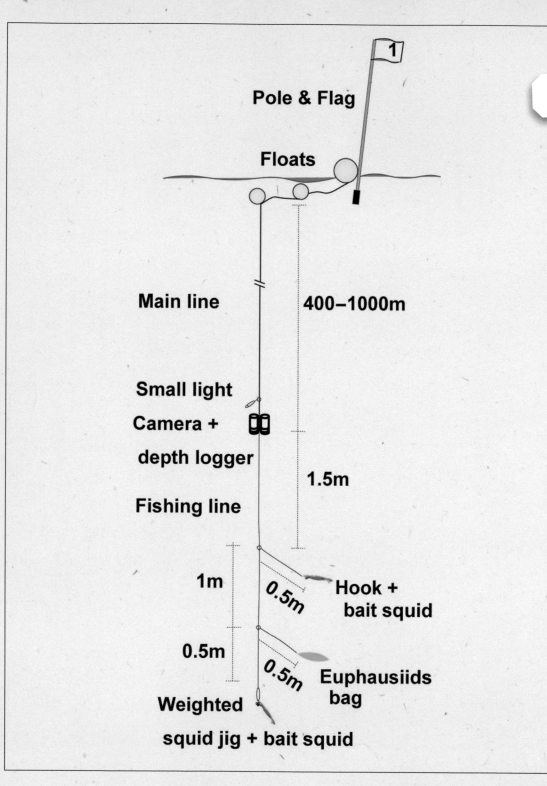

Pole & Flag

1

Floats

Main line 400–1000m

Small light

Camera +

depth logger 1.5m

Fishing line

1m

0.5m **Hook +
bait squid**

0.5m

0.5m **Euphausiids
bag**

Weighted

squid jig + bait squid

named Tsunemi Kubodera, were sure this was the best place to find the giant squid.

The Japanese scientists built a system they hoped would attract architeuthis. It consisted of a line more than three thousand feet long, outfitted with a camera and bait. The bait was made up of several small squid and some shrimp. This was hooked onto the line just below the camera. A light was attached to the line to provide illumination in the blackness of the ocean. Every thirty seconds, as it drifted deep in the water, the camera clicked a picture of the bait and anything else that happened to be nearby.

What the camera produced at 9:15 a.m. that September day was something that scientists and zoologists had dreamed about for hundreds of years.

At a depth of more than half a mile, a giant squid attacked the bait—in full view of the camera.

The squid loomed up in the lens, tentacles and arms first. It tried to rip the bait off the hooks but immediately snagged one of its tentacles. Unable to get free, it thrashed around the line, moving in and out of camera range. Over the course of four hours it attempted to get away as it shredded the bait and the camera clicked away. Finally, the architeuthis pulled the line so hard that it tore its tentacle right off. Then it sank back into the darkness.

When the researchers pulled the camera line back up, the tentacle was still snared on the hooks. And it was moving. It tried to grab parts of the boat and hands of the crew members who picked it up. According to Kubodera, "The recovered section of tentacle was still functioning, with the large suckers of the tentacle club repeatedly gripping the boat deck and any offered fingers."

The Japanese team took more than 550 photographs of the twenty-five-foot-long squid over the course of those four hours. It was an incredible achievement and a scientific first.

A member of Kubodera's crew handles the still moving section of tentacle.

Soon, the first pictures of a live *Architeuthis dux* were broadcast all over the world.

Some might have thought that Kubodera was lucky. No one really expected the first photographs of a live giant squid would be taken in the North Pacific Ocean—most specimens had been found in the North Atlantic or near Antarctica. But if it was true that Kubodera was lucky, then he was the luckiest squid searcher in history. Because a year after taking the first pictures of architeuthis live on camera, he got pictures of another architeuthis. This time, though, Kubodera got those pictures live on video.

Kubodera and his team dropped another line on January 27, 2006, near

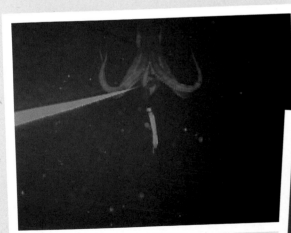

The first pictures of a live giant squid taken under water.

A live architeuthis rises to the surface!

line. It resisted attempts by the crew to pull it up on board. Though the researchers wanted desperately to save the giant squid, it died from the struggle. They returned to Japan with the body of this architeuthis and began studying it.

In the course of just over a year, the Japanese team had not only photographed a giant squid under the water, but had now videotaped one rising up to the surface. They had proved to the world that the giant squid could be found alive.

the island of Chichijima, about six hundred miles off the coast of Japan. Amazingly, another architeuthis took the bait. Once it had grabbed on, however, it wouldn't let go.

It became entangled in the line and the researchers pulled it to the surface. From their boat they filmed the squid as it rose up out of the water, its huge eyes staring up at them.

The red giant splashed savagely around the boat, fighting against the

The giant squid wrestles with the line.

This was everything that researchers had hoped for. To see the giant squid on film gave them new insight as to how the squid moved, how it attacked its prey, and what it looked like while it was alive. Most scientists never expected to see even this much in their lifetime.

But there was more to come. On January 8, 2007, Russian fishermen in the Ross Sea photographed a full-grown colossal squid. It had attacked fish that they were bringing up in their nets. The fisherman did not report what happened to the squid, but they did take several pictures to prove that they had seen it. This sighting of a living colossal squid—a creature much rarer than the giant squid—was cause for celebration.

That excitement was all but forgotten one month later. On February 22, 2007, while hauling up a line of Antarctic toothfish—again in the Ross Sea—fishermen on a boat from New Zealand named the *San Aspiring* discovered a colossal squid eating their fish. As the

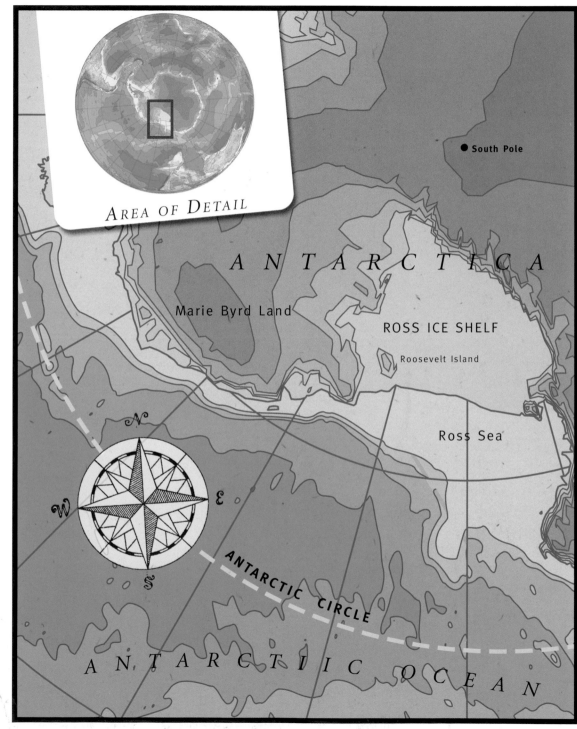

ANTARCTICA

AREA OF DETAIL

South Pole

ANTARCTICA

Marie Byrd Land

ROSS ICE SHELF

Roosevelt Island

Ross Sea

N

W   E

S

ANTARCTIC CIRCLE

ANTARCTIC OCEAN

fishermen brought the line to the surface, they could see the squid's huge, dark blood-colored body emerge from the black water. Determining that the squid was close to death—it made no attempt to escape—they decided to bring it up with a net. It took two hours of struggle to get it up on the ship.

They refrigerated the beast and transported it more than 1,500 miles back to New Zealand. It was the first full-grown colossal squid—and the largest cephalopod in history—ever seen by scientists. It weighed nearly one thousand pounds and was thirty-three feet long. It too went to the Museum of New Zealand, where it was immediately placed in a freezer and stored for more than a year. It took that long for Steve O'Shea and his team to determine how they would thaw the colossal squid without damaging it, and then how they would go about examining it. They needed to photograph

The fisherman hoist up the colossal squid from the freezing waters of the Ross Sea.

it, take tissue samples from it, and still leave most of it intact so that the squid could be displayed in the museum.

On April 28, 2008, the scientists were ready. The group included O'Shea, Kathrin Bolstad, and Tsunemi Kubodera, the man who had been the first to capture a giant squid live on film. Along with other international researchers, they began the slow task of defrosting the colossal squid. This was done by placing it in a huge water tank—big enough for the researchers to wade around in—and gradually melting the ice around the squid with

San Aspiring *captain John Bennett examines the historic catch.*

salt. Over the course of the next few days, they unfolded the squid from its icy block and with painstaking care they prodded, probed, and photographed the huge creature.

The world watched with awe as news cameras, a documentary film crew, reporters, and an Internet webcast captured the event, recording the researchers' progress. Images of a creature with the world's biggest eyes and lethal hooks on its arms and tentacles captured the imagination of people everywhere.

After thoroughly studying the mesonychoteuthis specimen, which the team determined was female, O'Shea injected it with formalin, a preservative that would keep the squid's body from deteriorating. The museum plans to display it in an 1,800-gallon tank—and it will be the only colossal squid on display anywhere in the world.

Most specimens of architeuthis and mesonychoteuthis have been kept in special freezers and labs in order to preserve them and give science a chance to look them over. Fortunately, there are squid specimens that have been put on display so that people interested in them can get a chance to view them up close. The first display was at Australia's Melbourne Aquarium in 2005. That squid had been caught by a fishing boat off the coast of New Zealand and was displayed in a three-ton block of ice, giving thousands of people the only glimpse they would ever have of architeuthis.

That same year, the London Natural History Museum transported a twenty-six-foot-long giant squid from the Falkland Islands off the coast of South America all the way to England. It was going to be the first display of a giant squid in Europe, the continent where the legend of the kraken was first told.

But because the body of the giant squid becomes fragile when it is out of the water, they had to be very careful with it. It had been frozen after it was caught and had to be defrosted once it got to the museum. The thick mantle would take longer to thaw than the thinner arms and tentacles, which were in danger of rotting before the rest of the creature thawed. It took three days to defrost, and then the appropriate tank needed to be built. The museum asked for advice from an artist named Damien Hirst, who is famous for his shocking museum displays of the bodies of sharks and cows in huge glass tanks. It took months to prepare the squid, nicknamed "Archie," before it was ready to be viewed by visitors to the museum.

Transporting massive squid is difficult because their bodies have to be infused with huge amounts of preservative. Unlike smaller specimens, which can be placed in tanks or tubs or bottles, these squid weigh hundreds of pounds. The chemicals that preserve them are very toxic, and there are restrictions on shipping those chemicals from country to country. Even then, getting approval to move the animals via airplane or ship is a complicated process. Researchers can't risk the containers getting delayed or damaged while being transported. If anything went wrong, the remains of the squid could rot and be ruined.

So the vast majority of giant and colossal squid specimens will remain in the hands of scientists as they try to learn all they can about these marvelous animals. There are some places you can see them, such as in the Museum of New Zealand. However, like the researchers who have spent their lives seeking these squid, you will most likely have to travel very far from your own home to see one.

In that small way, the myth of the kraken lives on. Only those who venture far out to sea will encounter the sight of this living creature with thrashing arms, a nasty odor, unblinking eyes, and tentacles lined with claws and teeth. Some things have not changed in more than a thousand years.

That brings us back to the beginning of the monster's story. The few people who *have* encountered the giant and colossal squid in the water tell tales of how amazing these sea creatures are, just as sailors did centuries ago. Scientists are awed by their size, their eyes, and the armature that lines their tentacles. The difference between then and now is that science has seen and studied the monster. We know that it is not a mythical creature, yet it remains a mysterious and magnificent beast. There is still much to learn about architeuthis and mesonychoteuthis. We don't know how they hunt their prey, or exactly how they reproduce, or how many offspring they have, or how they can remain hidden from us despite their great size, or why they sometimes choose to leave the dark and cold comfort of their ocean homes to come to the surface and enter our world.

The fact that we are just now seeing the giant and colossal squid alive in the water raises one last question about the legends of sea serpents. If it has taken us this long to come face-to-face with the mythical kraken, could there be other monsters—bigger ones—that we have yet to discover down at the bottom of the sea?

A photo of a colossal squid's head and eyes.

TRYING TO PHOTOGRAPH A PHANTOM

Although it is one of the largest creatures on earth, the giant squid has rarely been photographed alive. We have more close-up pictures of the surface of Mars than we do of live giant squids. Images of live colossal squids are even rarer.

It's amazing that we can send a robot vehicle more than thirty million miles to take pictures of Mars, yet we cannot get more pictures of a creature that lives just two miles below the watery surface of our own planet.

Fewer than a dozen giant and colossal squid have ever been photographed or filmed alive in the ocean. Almost every picture ever taken of living specimens is included in this book. And most of these were taken in a hurry, usually with a regular camera or video recorder. Remember, live giant and colossal squid have only been seen since 2006. Every single occasion that one appears is pretty amazing for everybody on the ship.

Because each squid sighting was unexpected, researchers did not have the opportunity to set up a nice photo shoot where they could pose the squid or wait to get the best picture possible. Every second counted, and they had to get pictures of whatever they could, using whatever cameras were at hand. Taking the photos was not an easy task, since the people holding the cameras were standing on the deck of a moving boat and the squid were usually bobbing up and down and in and out of the ocean waves.

Thus, some of the pictures of live squid in this book are smaller or fuzzier than those taken in a lab. Even with modern technology, the whole world is still waiting for that one truly amazing shot of a live giant squid as it moves through the ocean water.

ACKNOWLEDGMENTS

Everyone who writes about or researches an exciting subject owes a debt to the writing and research that have come before. Sir Isaac Newton, one of the greatest scientists in history, called this "standing on the shoulders of giants." I am indebted to the giants who have done extraordinary work on both *Architeuthis dux* and *Mesonychoteuthis hamiltoni* over the past several decades. First and foremost, I want to thank Clyde Roper, Steve O'Shea, and Kat Bolstad for the significant amount of time and effort they each spent helping me to understand the nuances of these fascinating animals. Each of them provided me with information, photographs, and bits of trivia that have helped to make this book much more interesting than it would have been without them.

I also want to thank Tsunemi Kubodera of the National Science Museum in Tokyo for his input and for the original photographs he took of the live giant squid. Much gratitude goes to Eric Lazo-Wasem of the Peabody Museum at Yale University for walking me through Yale's giant squid history and allowing me to get up close and personal with the university's architeuthis specimens.

Thanks also to the staffs of the American Museum of Natural History in New York, the Te Papa Museum in Wellington, New Zealand, the Melbourne Aquarium in Melbourne, Victoria, Australia, and the Smithsonian Institution in Washington, D.C., for providing me with information and photographs.

The book you are holding in your hand would not have been possible if not for the input of a great many people. An ocean of gratitude goes to Kate O'Sullivan, my editor and fellow monster enthusiast, for her keen interest in the stranger side of nature; Scott Magoon and Greta Sibley, who worked diligently on the artwork and layout; and my agent, Ken Wright, who keeps finding exactly the right homes for my writing. Thanks to Madeline Newquist and Katherine Newquist for Web research, proofing, and line editing.

Finally, a tentacle's embrace to the people who provided support and inspiration along the way: my parents, my brothers and sisters and their families, Michael and Barbara Johnson, Thomas Werge, John Kunkel (RIP), Tucker Greco and family, Rich Maloof and family, Pete Prown and family, Bill Brahos and family, Bill Leary, Al Mowrer, Bill McGuinness, Peter Fitzpatrick, Lynne and Tim Carlson, Sammy Cemo and family, bandmates past and present, and all those who make it enjoyable to discuss and explore brand-new things. Most especially that means Trini, Madeline, and Katherine . . . because they are there with me each and every day.

Thank you for taking the time to read this book. You can find out more about me and my other books at www.newquist books.com. I hope what you've read in these pages made you think, and perhaps inspired you. Always remember that the world is a splendid place, and it's waiting for you.

HP Newquist

Researchers get into the tank to study the colossal squid in New Zealand

BIBLIOGRAPHY

There have been very few books written about *Architeuthis dux*. The following two are viewed as the best early works on the giant squid, even though they were written before there were any photos or video of a live giant squid. These books provide fascinating insight into a time when the creature itself was emerging from myth into reality:

In the Wake of the Sea-Serpents by Bernard Heuvelmans. Translated by Richard Garnett. (New York: Hill and Wang, 1968)

The Search for the Giant Squid by Richard Ellis (New York: Lyons Press, 1998)

FOR FURTHER RESEARCH

There are a great number of places to go on the Web for more information about the giant and colossal squid—and it is being updated all the time. In fact, as this book was being printed in late 2009, the U.S. government reported that a giant squid had been accidentally captured in a net in the Gulf of Mexico—the first time architeuthis had been spotted in that area in more than fifty years. Things are changing all the time in the mysterious world of the giant squid, so it's worth looking for more updates on the Internet.

Here are some excellent sites to check out.

Clyde Roper's first expedition to find the Giant Squid, based on the Smithsonian National Museum of Natural History exhibit "In Search of Giant Squids":
seawifs.gsfc.nasa.gov/OCEAN_PLANET/
HTML/squid_opening.html
www.mnh.si.edu/natural_partners/
squid4/Default.html

A Japanese film of a live giant squid:
www.freesciencelectures.com/video/
giant-squid-caught-on-film/

Steve O'Shea's fact sheet about Colossal and Giant Squids:
www.tonmo.com/science/public/giantsquidfacts.php

Te Papa's pages on the defrosting of the colossal squid and the creation of its permanent home for the squid:
blog.tepapa.govt.nz/category/colossal-squid/

Colossal squid website:
www.tepapa.govt.nz/TePapa/English/
CollectionsAndResearch/Collection-
Areas/NaturalEnvironment/Molluscs/
ColossalSquid/

PHOTO CREDITS

INDEX

Page numbers in **bold type** refer to illustrations.

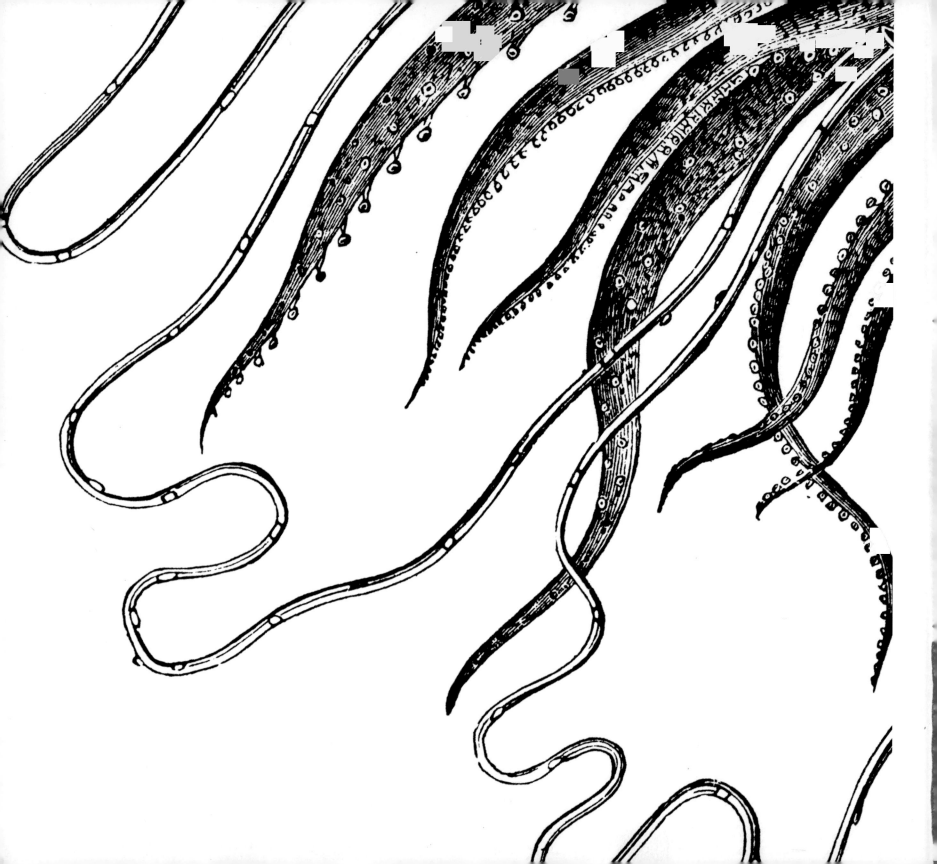